I0169221

Slave of Two Masters

Slave of Two Masters

Melinda Selmys

Vulgata

Scripture citations are taken from the Jerusalem Bible, copyright 1966 by Darton, Longman and Todd Ltd., & Doubleday and Company Inc.

To the best of my knowledge, all copyrighted works referenced in this book have been quoted in accord with accepted standards of fair use. If you are a copyright holder amd I have used your work in a way that you don't like, or have presumed excessively on your generosity, please notify me so that the problem may be rectified in future printings.

© Melinda Selmys, 2013

Some rights reserved.

This work is licensed under the Creative Commons Attribution-NonCommercial-ShareAlike 3.0 Unported License. To view a copy of this license, visit

http://creativecommons.org/licenses/by-nc-sa/3.0/.

ISBN 978-0-9919098-0-3

for Theresa

◦ **CONTENTS** ◦

INTRODUCTION

To suffer and to endure...is the lot of humanity; let them strive as they may, no strength and no artifice will ever succeed in banishing from human life the ills and troubles which beset it.

Rerum Novarum

There is a refrain that runs through Scripture from Genesis through to Revelation: money is not reliable. Man, in earthly life, labors under a curse: "With sweat on your brow shall you eat your bread" (Gen 3:19). The soil will bring forth thistles. Drought and famine will destroy crops. Moths and woodworms will eat up your treasures. Thieves will break in and steal your riches (see Matt 6:19-21). Just as you've finally amassed all that you need to be happy and live comfortably for the rest of your life, death will come stalking at the door, demanding your soul. As Christ warns the two brothers who are fighting over an inheritance, "Watch, and be on your guard against avarice of any kind, for a man's life is not made secure by what he owns, even when he has more than he needs" (Luke 12:15).

It is therefore necessary to put to death the notion that money can bring the joy and peace which human beings desire. It is not possible to worship the Lord God of Israel, but also, just a little bit, to worship the golden calf. Even if you convince yourself that worshiping the golden calf is just a way of honoring the Lord God of Israel — as the Israelites did — the covenant will be broken, and God will turn away His face.

Does this mean that Christians must live a life of grim austerity, feasting on ashes, dressed in sackcloth, weeping and tearing their beards all the days of their lives? Must we forgo all earthly joys for the promise of bliss in another world? Only if we assume that the enjoyment of earthly life must be measured in gold.

Let's begin by asking why it is that people desire wealth. Is it not because they believe that it will make them happy? Why do they desire financial security? Is it not so that they may live without anxiety and fear? Surely if we were given a magic goat, as in the fairy tales, and all we had to do was reach into its ear each morning and pull out a tablecloth spread with every good thing, we would happily do without money. Having attained the end, we would readily dispense with the means.

Before we turn away sad, as the rich young man did, we might consider whether money even has the benefits that people wish to derive from it. Do the things that people buy make them happy? Does the pursuit of financial security actually free people from worry and anxieties? Christ argues that it does not: "a man's life is not made secure by what he owns." As a means of attaining happiness and peace of mind, money continually disappoints. Why, then, should anyone be saddened by the prospect of giving it up?

ADAM'S CURSE

Creation constitutes the fundamental and original gift: man appears in creation as the one who has received the world as a gift, and vice versa, one can also say that the world has received man as a gift.

John Paul II

In the Beginning, there was no scarcity. Adam and Eve lived together in the Garden of Eden, cultivating the earth and taking care of it. "God caused to spring up from the soil every kind of tree, enticing to look at and good to eat" (Gen 2:9). The earth yielded readily to their labors. They were at peace with one another and with the whole order of creation.

We no longer live in that paradise. At the threshold of history, Eve suffered a temptation. The Serpent appeared in the garden and directed her eyes towards the fruit of the tree of the knowledge of good and evil, and she "saw that the tree was good to eat and pleasing to the eye, and that it was desirable for the knowledge that it could give" (Gen 3:6). Lured by the promise of these pleasures and by the Serpent's comforting patter, she ate. She offered some of the fruit to Adam, and he also partook of the forbidden fig.

Although Scripture gives a detailed description of Eve's psychology at the moment of the temptation, it is silent about what is going through Adam's head. His sin is described in a single clause: "and he ate it" (Gen 3:6). However, when God asks Adam why he ate, he replies, "It was the woman you put with me" (Gen 3:12). Adam fingers Eve. The woman, who was supposed to be his helpmate, becomes an adversary, a temptress who led him down the path

3

to destruction, and also a scapegoat, someone whom he can blame for his misdeeds. The opening volley in the war of the sexes has just been fired. Eve, unwilling to accept responsibility, turns on the Serpent. We are not told how the Serpent replied; we can probably assume that he smiled.

God was not convinced by Adam and Eve's excuses, so He cursed them. Adam got hard labor, Eve got pain in childbirth, and the Serpent was sentenced to crawl on his belly. Very traditional punishments: the chain gang, the rack, and public humiliation. Yet there is a deeper and more mysterious dimension which often gets missed. Eve was also punished with desire for her husband, who would lord it over her; for the Serpent there was to be enmity with the woman. The relationships that had been broken in the course of the Fall would remain broken. These curses were not arbitrary punishments but the natural consequences of the sin which Adam and Eve committed.

What was this sin? The theologians tell us that it was the sin of Pride, and this is true. Some people have tried to argue that it was Lust. This is also true. Contained in that original sin were all the sins of men: pride first, but also all of the other evils which proceed from pride. Here, I would like to talk about it as a sin of Avarice.

Adam and Eve had been given the earth as a gift. The gift was not, however, given without limit: God withheld something. "You may eat indeed of all the trees in the garden. Nevertheless of the tree of the knowledge of good and evil you are not to eat" (Gen 2:17). The Serpent came along, and the first thing that he did was to suggest that God was being stingy: "Did God really say you were not to eat from any of the trees in the garden?" (Gen 3:1). The serpent seems to be saying, "Hey, isn't God keeping something back from you? Why would He do that?" Eve's attention is now directed towards the one tree that God has forbidden. Here she stands, surrounded by the original beauty of creation, with good food hanging from every branch. We've already been told that all of the trees are enticing and all are good to eat from, but now Eve can only see one: the one that she does not possess.

She snatches the forbidden fruit and shares it with her husband. Suddenly the earth is no longer a gift: it is plunder. In seizing what is not theirs, Adam and Eve display contempt for the good things that God has given them. God honors this new arrangement. Now the earth will hold back her wealth. "It shall yield you brambles and thistles, and you shall eat wild plants. With sweat on your brow shall you eat your bread, until you return to the soil, as you were taken from it. For dust you are and to dust you shall return" (Gen 3:18-19). From now on Adam will have to work hard for the things which used to be free, and no matter how hard he works, he might gain nothing for his effort but sweat and thistle stew.

Eve's avarice will also be punished, but it will be punished through Adam. He will no longer treat her as a helpmate, an equal in dignity and a partner in his work. Instead he will "lord it over her." Their interests are no longer identical, and Adam, being the stronger of the two, will turn her from a helper into a possession. This relationship will not only characterize the relations of the sexes but all human relationships — including those essential to economic life. Everywhere men shall be born free, and everywhere they shall put one another into chains. Our parents plundered the earth, they turned against each other, and they tried to conceal their theft by hiding from God. In doing so, they created a new economic model for all generations. Every man who looks at his neighbor's goods and, seeing that they are pleasing and desirable, reaches out to take more than his share will suffer the same fate. No economic system, social ideology, financial scheme, or new technology will ever save us from this curse.

WOMAN'S WORK

One day, all human accomplishments will be reduced to a pile of ashes. But every single child to whom a woman has given birth will live forever, for he has been given an immortal soul made to God's image and likeness.

Alice von Hildebrand

God's punishments are very appropriate. Eve hoped to have the serpent punished in her place, so God punished the serpent in a way that harmed Eve. The enmity between them would continue to plague Eve's offspring right through to the end times (see Rev 12:1-6). Adam tried to push the blame off on Eve, so God punished Eve in a way that afflicted Adam.

Adam might have thought that he was getting the long end of the stick when God declared that he would "lord it over" Eve, but John Paul II thought differently: "If a man relates to a woman in such a way that he considers her only as an object to appropriate and not as a gift, he condemns himself at the same time to become, on his part too, only an object of appropriation for her and not a gift. It seems that the words of Genesis 3:16 deal with this two-sided relationship" (*Theology of the Body*).

Once Eve was cursed to have Adam "lord it over her," which aspects of human endeavor did he choose for himself? It is usually assumed that Adam took the better portion and left the dregs to Eve — and certainly men have seen it this way over the centuries. They assumed responsibility for the sciences, the arts, politics, economic life, invention, production, and all of the truly important tasks that contribute to the building up of civilization. Women, oddly enough, have readily accepted that these are indeed the essential human activities; as Simone de Beauvoir complained, "women produce nothing."

But what is it that women produce? Men, arrogantly desiring to claim all of the credit for human achievement, have habitually missed the glaring and inescapable fact that women produce men. Society, economics, science, culture, knowledge, politics, and production are all just things that serve human interests; only human persons are ends in themselves. If men have believed that bearing and caring for rational beings is a purely biological act, fitting only for the delicate and weak-minded, it is because their priorities have become seriously warped.

What men chose for themselves is not the better part of human achievement but the more ostentatious part. In "lording it over" women they have clutched at those aspects of human achievement which are outside of the person and which are therefore most likely to enslave the soul to external desires. The dregs which have traditionally been left to women are the activities which are centered in the dignity of the human person rather than in the grandeur of his accomplishments. The stone of women's labor, which the builders of Western civilization have rejected, is indeed the cornerstone.

This has dire consequences for a society in which not only men but also women have rejected women's work in favor of economic accomplishment. John Paul II, in *Mulieris Dignitatem*, suggests that the increased participation of women in social, economic, and cultural life could serve to positively transform those areas in the light of "women's genius." Yet this can be accomplished only if women's genius itself is preserved — and that genius is intimately connected to motherhood.

The economics of motherhood is governed by very different principles than the economics of the marketplace. In domestic life, the stronger do not triumph, or even seek to triumph, over the weak. "If there is only a crust of bread in the house, and mother and children are starving, their interests are not the same. If the mother eats it, the children want it; if the children eat it, the mother must go hungry to her work. Yet it does not necessarily follow that there will be 'antagonism' between them, that they will fight for the crust, and that the mother, being strongest, will get it, and eat it" (John Ruskin). Both Ruskin and John Paul II expressed a hope that it would be possible to reform economics so that it could be fueled by such an engine of love and affection, rather than being governed solely by self-interest.

Sadly, what has happened instead is that women have become increasingly enslaved to those same external accomplishments that have always obsessed men. Classical feminists, with all of the best of intentions, often assumed that the quality of a woman's life could be measured by the acquisition of wealth and that the primary problems facing women are wage inequality and lack of access to higher paying positions. These are certainly problems, particularly when the poverty of women is so often shared with their children; however, when mothers complain about the life of a housewife, or of a single mother, their primary complaint is not poverty but loneliness. This loneliness is the result of the loss of a sense of value for the work that women have always done, the loss of space where this work can take place, and the loss of a community that works together to support this work. Speaking to women from Africa and India, I have repeatedly come across the same refrain: "It is easy to have a lot of children in my country. It is very difficult here."

Ironically, in trying to escape from the curse laid on Eve, women have succeeded in exacerbating it. They have entered into the world of toil and sweat. They are now privileged to be paid meager wages and to be taxed for their work. They still work for men, and the men still lord it over them. Their fertility is artificially suppressed, their bodies freely available for sex. They have been inducted into the male-dominated worship of that golden idol in the temple of Mammon and have lost the dignity of being the tabernacle of the image and likeness of God.

MONEY, MONEY

The just distribution of material things is not merely a problem of technique or of organization. It is primarily a moral problem.

Richard B. Gregg

What is money? The obvious answer is that money is a means of exchange, a handy way of overcoming the inconveniences of the barter system. Originally, valuable goods were exchanged for equally valuable metals; gold weighed less than cattle, and its value was universally recognized, so it could be traded for anything. The sort of fiat money that we are familiar with today would have seemed alien, probably even frightening, to ancient man: on what basis would he have faith in the power of this token? Once he had given up his cow for a bit of colored paper, why would someone else be willing to take the paper in exchange for a cow?

Money is an abstraction of value. It is also a promise: implicit in the conversion of goods to money is the assurance that the abstraction can once more be made concrete. It is, in this way, similar to language: a word is both an abstraction of a concrete thing, and also a sign that points back towards that thing. Both words and money can be made to lie. If I say "There is plenty to eat in the cupboard," and there is not plenty to eat, the words have been made to signify a reality that is not there. If someone's life or freedom of action is dependent on the existence of the thing that is not there, then the lie assumes true moral gravity: it not only offends against truth, but also harms the person who believes the lie. If someone produces money that does not correspond to any genuine value, this is the financial equivalent of lying — and since money is generally used to vouchsafe the value of human labor and the ability to procure the means of survival, it is a grave lie indeed.

Financial gurus perennially point out that "rich people don't work for their money; they make their money work for them." What they mean is either one of two things:

1. Rich people buy up the means of production and charge other people for the right to use them.

2. Rich people lend their money at interest and make a profit from usury.

Both of these practices are problematic. The first violates the principle of private property because it tends to concentrate ownership in the hands of the few. "The *right to private property*, acquired or received in a just way, does not do away with the original gift of the earth to the whole of mankind. The *universal destination of goods* remains primordial, even if the promotion of the common good requires respect for the right to private property and its exercise" (CCC 2403). The Vatican is very clear in emphasizing that the right to private property is not a right to amass property at the expense of others, but rather a universal right which is best realized when the maximum possible number of people are enabled to share in ownership, for "every man has by nature the right to possess property as his own" (*Rerum Novarum*). This is a point that we will return to later.

Usury poses even greater problems. It is condemned in the Old Testament, particularly in relation to the poor: "If you lend money to any of my people, to any poor man among you, you must not play the usurer with him: you must not demand interest from him" (Exod 22:25). Until the Middle Ages, the Church forbade lending at interest, and today the Vatican continues to plead for the forgiveness of usurious debts which enslave individuals and nations.

Usury subtly changes the nature of money so that it ceases to express values that actually exist, and comes to express debt. It is a promise that something of value will come into being in the future. This kind of promise lacks integrity because it offers what it does not yet possess. A man who promises to bring his love back the heart of a dragon means that he will try to bring his love back the heart of a dragon, that he earnestly desires to do so, and will make an honest effort. It by no means ensures that a dragon's heart will ever actually manifest on his lady's table. It is a very different sort of promise than the promise to give himself lovingly to his lady for the rest of his life: a promise which he may make because he is already in possession of himself, and may certainly expect to continue in such self-possession until his death.

The condemnation of usury does not preclude speculative investment. The difference between usury and legitimate forms of investment is that the usurer is being paid for the use of his money, and he expects to get his money back, with interest, regardless of whether his debtor is able to pay. An investor joins his wealth to someone else's project in the anticipation that the venture will succeed. He does not get a return on his investment, or even recoup his capital, unless his wealth is used to produce something of real value.

Usury on a private scale has caused countless social ills: indentured slavery, debtors prisons, and violent debt collections. On a public scale, it is catastrophic. The recent banker bail-outs are a case in point: the economic stability of the United States depended on the value of usurious loans which were made in bad faith. When it did not prove possible to redeem these debts, it was necessary to commit a universal robbery — to pay for the mistakes of the rich by taking money from the middle class and the poor. Such injustices are endemic to societies in which usury is the norm.

VANITY, VANITY

The present world is a theater, the conditions of men are roles: wealth and poverty, ruler and ruled, and so forth....When the masks are removed, then the truly rich and the truly poor are revealed.

Saint John Chrysostom

The greatest danger that money poses is that it ceases to have anything to do with the value of goods at all, and becomes a way of measuring the value of a human life. Why do people abort their children? Often, it is because they feel they don't have enough money to support a child. Why are the elderly abandoned in warehouse-style hospital wards, lonely and ignored while they wait in quiet desperation for death? Because they are "useless," no longer able to financially contribute to the world.

Even those who are not personally responsible for macroeconomic injustices will be influenced by the fact that they live in a society whose economy flourishes in the soil of injustice. "A theory that makes profit the exclusive norm and ultimate end of economic activity is morally unacceptable. The disordered desire for money cannot but produce perverse effects. It is one of the causes of the many conflicts which disturb the social order" (*Gaudium et Spes*). When wealth is divorced from the genuine value of real goods, this divorce produces a whole wealth of microeconomic perversions.

In consumer capitalism, money becomes the abstract form of a cultural fantasy of perpetual growth, endlessly increasing profit, and the infinite multiplication of goods. This fantasy is acted out not only on Wall Street, but also in the lives of individuals. It is not wealth but the fantasy of wealth, not value but the appearance of value that becomes important. This fuels the need not only for more and more consumer goods, but also for consumer goods that confer status and identity on the person who owns them — what social thinkers frequently refer to as "conspicuous consumption."

Conspicuous consumption takes a number of different forms. Thorstein Veblen observed that some goods are perceived to be of greater value simply because their price is high. Diamonds are a good example: they are actually a fairly common stone, but because De Beers has monopolistic control over the supply they have been able to create artificial scarcity and keep the prices high. The value of a diamond is almost entirely a product of its price; it is not especially attractive compared to other gems, and it is not particularly rare. A woman wants to receive a diamond because it ostentatiously demonstrates that her lover or husband was willing and able to spend a lot of money to buy her a piece of jewelry. This is why one of the primary pleasures associated with owning a diamond is showing it off to others. Fancy cars, designer clothing, and expensive watches are other common examples of "Veblen goods."

Philosopher Jean Baudrillard made a similar observation about the use of material goods as symbols of immaterial values. He noted that any given material object has two different kinds of value: it has a use value (the amount of utility which can be derived from the good), and it has a sign value (a value based on what the object means to the person who owns it.) Advertisers constantly attempt to increase the amount that people will pay for products by infusing them with artificial sign value. Emotional branding, for example, is the practice of using images to link a product with a positive emotional state, so that people will unthinkingly purchase the product when they crave the emotion. Baudrillard points out that this is not entirely unsuccessful. Although a pair of shoes cannot offer real self-confidence, they may be able to give a person the illusion or simulation of self-confidence. Over time, as real spiritual goods are replaced with their simulations, people come to doubt the value of the genuine goods, and even to believe that the simulacra are the real thing.

In the present age, one of the immaterial values which material things are often called on to signify is identity. Marshal McLuhan described the world today as "not a global village, but a global theater." Television creates a culture in which people often have stronger relationships with artificial characters than with other human beings and in which role models are very often people who are themselves playing a role. Identities are no longer rooted in families or in communities, and the anonymity of city life creates a need to create and maintain identities which are immediately visible and which declare themselves through concrete symbols. Consumer goods become the tribal signs by which people with similar interests and attitudes recognize and identify one another. In many sub-cultures, the outward signs of wealth, success, or fashion are essential to defining oneself as an insider, and even in "counter-cultural" circles, it is often necessary to live in the right neighborhood, to eat from the right grocery stores, and to participate in the consumption of niche-marketed goods.

When people buy their identities on the free market the result is always self-consciousness and anxiety. The loss of the ability to participate in consumption literally involves a loss of the sense of self. In this context, people will do anything to secure the ability to maintain their consumer identities and avoid the stigmatization and loss of a sense of personal value associated with poverty.

Conspicuous consumption is not only a good way to make oneself poor fast, it is also immoral: "Countless millions are starving, countless families are destitute, countless men are steeped in ignorance; countless people need schools, hospitals, and homes worthy of the name. In such circumstances, we cannot tolerate public and private expenditures of a wasteful nature; we cannot but condemn lavish displays of wealth by nations or individuals" *(Populorum Progressio)*.

WASTE NOT

There must be a reason why some people can afford to live well.
They must have worked for it. I only feel angry when I see waste.
When I see people throwing away things that we could use.

Mother Teresa

The great boon which capitalism was supposed to bring to the world was a more efficient system for the production of goods and the employment of human labor. Traditional capitalist thinkers like Adam Smith believed that capitalism would be good for laborers as well as capitalists, because it would make possible the production of more and better products with less time and effort expended.

Aristotle would have approved — at least in principle. He asserted that the purpose of civilization was to free people from the necessity of laboring to produce the necessities of life and to create leisure. This does not mean that Aristotle fancied that the purpose of civilization was to produce the greatest number of couchpotatoes. Aristotle meant by "leisure" the freedom to develop one's intellect and character. Indeed, he considered it "inconceivable" that "amusement would be the end [purpose] of life" (Aristotle). People possessed of leisure are freed to pursue the arts and sciences, to build up culture, and to collectively pursue the good life.

Industrialism, mechanization, and capitalism were supposed to increase leisure and eliminate toil by replacing human slaves with mechanical ones, and to eliminate waste by directly matching supply to demand. The fatal flaw: "Some persons are led to believe that getting wealth is the object of household management, and the whole idea of their lives is

18

that they ought either to increase their money without limit, or at any rate not lose it. The origin of this disposition in men is that they are intent upon living only, and not upon living well; and, as their desires are unlimited, they also desire that the means of gratifying them should be without limit" (Aristotle).

The time freed by industrial processes has not, by and large, become time for leisure activities, but rather time for the acquisition and production of money and of goods beyond the rational needs of a human being. Instead of matching supply to demand, consumerism seeks to create artificial demands in order to justify a limitless increase in supply. It is not merely that ordinary people have unlimited desires which the machinery of industry seeks to alleviate, but rather that the people who own the machinery of industry have an unlimited desire to profit from the goods that they produce, and therefore must inculcate desire in marketplace.

The simplest way to increase demand is to create products which are made to be wasted. Disposable goods are associated with "convenience," which, like efficiency, is supposed to liberate time. This however is very often an illusion accomplished through sleight of hand: the worker, having already spent time in order to gain money, no longer sees the intimate connection between the money gained and the time spent. In many cases, the amount of time that is saved by a convenience product is not comparable with the amount of effort that it takes to earn the money to purchase it.

The disposable culture is one which deeply insults the gift of the earth to man. People, instead of being stewards of material wealth, become consumers: literally devouring teeth which grind up the riches of the earth and are never satisfied. But not the earth alone suffers. In a disposable economy, not only goods but also human beings become disposable.

Slavery in the present age is not called slavery, but many people have shrewdly observed that it is possible to enslave people without chains or slave auctions. "It too often happens, however, even in our day, that in one way or another workers are made slaves of their work" (*Gaudium et Spes*). If a person has no way of getting the basic means of sustenance for himself and his family except through submission to unjust labor conditions, then he is *de facto* a slave. Wage slavery is the practice of keeping wages low enough that the laborer cannot afford to sustain himself and is forced to go into debt in order to buy necessities — usually into debt to the same people who employ his labor. People in poor countries and migrant workers in wealthy countries often live under these conditions so that people in rich countries are able to enjoy rock-bottom prices, while the laborers who make our goods are not paid a living wage.

The difference between traditional slavery and enslavement through unjust economic practices is that the slave is valuable to his master. The master has made an investment in this person, and will lose something if the slave is overworked or otherwise rendered useless. There is also generally a relationship between the two. The master feels at least some sense of responsibility and will usually continue to support slaves who have become too old to work. Wage slavery on the other hand, produces disposable slaves. There is no relationship, no sense of responsibility, and when the worker can no longer work they are simply dismissed. The employer does not pursue any interest in what becomes of them after that.

When men treat the fruits of the earth and of human labor with contempt, disposing of them instead of valuing and maintaining them, they treat one another with contempt. Recall that Adam in appropriating the fruit also came to see Eve as an object of appropriation. Ingratitude for the gifts of the earth prepares the soul to be ungrateful also for the gift of other human beings. This is a large part of why our present society, not in spite of but because of its affluence, is a culture of loneliness.

NOT WASTE

For what is thought highly of by men is loathsome in the sight of God.

Luke 16:15

Objects bind time. Every product that is ever manufactured is a manifestation of the time that was spent making it, and also of the time that was spent earning the money to buy it. Goods should therefore be manufactured in a way that respects and values the time of the people who make them. Often, for the sake of profit, goods are deliberately engineered to break after only a limited period of use by a practice called "planned obsolescence." This demonstrates a lack of respect for human labor: people have a natural desire to produce quality goods that will last. The deliberate multiplication of goods which are cheap, frivolous, or poorly made deprives laborers of their pride of workmanship and employs their time in a manner that is not in accord with human dignity.

Although manufacturers are primarily responsible for producing quality products, consumers are not without guilt. There are many wasteful consumer practices which drive the demand for large supplies of poorly made products. Many people like to shop even when they do not actually need to buy anything. This often results in the purchase of goods which a person doesn't actually want to own but which they take pleasure in acquiring. Low-quality "bargains" are ideal for this purpose, because they produce the illusion of frugality. The compulsive shopper is able to congratulate himself on such purchases on the basis that he got a good deal. Shopping in this way is not only a waste of one's own time, it is also a waste of time for the people who had to make the rubbish that is bought.

Another reason that manufacturers are able to get away with "optimizing" items to break down quickly is that shoppers are addicted to novelty. The practice of "planned obsolescence" would not be acceptable to a consumer base that valued quality and durability. Consumers have, however, been trained to attach sign value to ownership of the latest models of most goods. Companies are therefore able to engineer products that will expire years, or sometimes decades, earlier than they need to because more often than not the customer will be bored with the product by the time it breaks.

Manufacturers cannot produce quality goods or pay their laborers a just wage unless people are willing to pay a fair price for the things that they wish to own. Paul VI suggested that Catholics ought to be "prepared to pay more for imported goods, so that the foreign producer may make a fairer profit" (*Populorum Progressio*). Cheaply manufactured mass-market commodities with "Made in China" or "Manufactured in Indonesia" on the label are practically guaranteed to be the fruit of human exploitation. Those who can afford locally grown foods, goods made in countries with reasonable labor laws, and "fair trade" products have an obligation to buy responsibly, even if it means owning fewer things. Critics might point out that an ethically manufactured product might rely on unethically obtained materials. This is a flimsy excuse. If it is impossible to achieve moral perfection, one must not conclude that all moral effort is futile; nor should the fact that perfect economic justice is unattainable prevent anyone from acting more justly.

Not everyone can afford to buy high quality goods made under ethical conditions, but those who cannot can still stem the wastage of human time by reclaiming the wealth which others waste. According to John Hoffman, author of *The Art and Science of Dumpster Diving*, "Sooner or later just about anything will be thrown out. Whatever your concern, whatever your interest, somebody is probably tossing out something you can use right this minute." The objects that populate our landfill sites are manifestations of human time and labor, and keeping them out of the dump is a responsible way of reasserting the dignity of the human person. Many people will see something on the road-side that they need and will not pick it up because they fear the stigma of appearing to be poor. This is foolish. God does not want to see the goods of the earth wasted, and He should not be prevented from providing for us in this way. Some people will raise the objection that it is immoral to "steal" something from someone else's garbage. This is not true: winnowing someone's discarded goods does not violate the "reasonable will of the owner" (CCC 2408). However, those who have this scruple may simply ask permission. Human beings have an inborn conscientious desire not to be wasteful, and most people are relieved to know that the things which they can no longer use are going to "a good home."

Responsible stewardship of goods also demands that people treat their own property with respect. Everything that a person owns is a gift from God, bought with human time and human labor. People have an obligation to ensure that their possessions continue to bring value and joy to the human race for as long as possible. Ending is not better than mending. Repairing broken goods is a way of honoring the people who made them. Often those who are skilled at repairing engines or electronics will happily accept donations of mildly damaged goods; sometimes people who have these skills will do the repairs and then hand the refurbished products on to those in need. If a person owns something which they no longer need, someone else probably does need it. It is culpable sloth to throw good things in the trash without making a reasonable attempt to give them away. The

Catechism specifically lists waste as amongst the sins against the sixth commandment (2409), and responsible ownership is a moral obligation that corresponds to the universal destination of goods.

FILTHY LUCRE

Every country, rich or poor, has a cultural tradition handed down from past generations. This tradition includes institutions required by life in the world, and higher manifestations — artistic, intellectual and religious — of the life of the spirit. When the latter embody truly human values, it would be a great mistake to sacrifice them for the sake of the former. Any group of people who would consent to let this happen, would be giving up the better portion of their heritage; in order to live, they would be giving up their reason for living. Christ's question is directed to nations also: "What does it profit a man, if he gain the whole world but suffer the loss of his own soul?"

Populorum Progressio

Corrupt. Degraded. Filthy. Lucre. Mammon. Some interpreters try to say that it's only ill-gotten money that is designated "filthy lucre" or "unrighteous mammon," but the surrounding text really doesn't give this impression. The note on Luke 16:9 in the Jerusalem Bible observes that "Money is here called 'tainted' not only because its owner is here presumed to have gained it dishonestly but because great wealth is rarely acquired without some sharp practice." It might reasonably be added that even if the individual is not guilty of any dishonesty, money that circulates through any economy is likely to have derived a certain amount of its value from corporate sin: the guilt associated with unjust foreign policies, rapacious tax practices, predatory international loans, or other macroeconomic evils.

Yet there seems to be another sense in which money is "tainted." Christ draws a parallel between two different kinds of value: "If then you cannot be trusted with money, that tainted thing, who will trust you with genuine riches?" (Luke 16:11). Christ is using money as a symbol for all human commerce, material goods, and objects of worldly desire. He says that money is "not yours"(Luke 16:12), an observation which points us towards the universal destination of goods, "In the beginning God entrusted the earth and its resources to the common stewardship of mankind to take care of them, master them by labor and enjoy their fruits. The goods of creation are destined for the whole human race" (CCC 2402). In contrast, He speaks of "genuine riches" which are "your very own" (Luke 16:12). It's clear that He is drawing a distinction between goods that are external to the human person, which are ultimately corruptible, and goods that are interior, the "treasure in heaven" that cannot be corrupted or destroyed.

The corruptibility of worldly goods is a manifestation of their relationship with humanity. Things in the natural world do not possess innate value. This is not to say that their value is not real, but that their value does not come from within themselves. Valuation is an act of the will: no one looks at a thing and apprehends its value; rather one looks at a thing and assigns value to it. We choose to value or not to value the objects that we encounter. A tree, being incapable of making acts of will, is not able to value itself; therefore its value comes from without and is determined by the person who observes and makes decisions about it. It might be valued for its beauty, for the cool shade that it provides, or for the goods that could be made from its wood; or it might have negative value and be perceived as a pest which leeches goodness out of the soil and casts shade over the potato plants. These values originate in a person, not in the material thing itself.

God has given the Earth to human beings as a gift because there are unique ways in which a human being can value material things. An angel cannot, for example, value a swimming pool because it keeps him cool in the heat of the day. Human beings, in interacting with and assigning values to things that we encounter, enrich the Earth with new meanings and significances: we increase its value by interacting with it.

These values are not solely subjective. A human agent by assigning value to a material thing impresses that value on it. A relationship is established between the object and the person. If this relationship is ordered, that is, if the person owns the object without being owned by it, then the object becomes a means of attaining perfection. Its purpose within the order of creation is fulfilled, and although the object itself will pass away, the significance with which it was invested — a significance which has made its imprint on the heart of a human subject — will endure. In other words, by valuing a thing, a person loves a thing and gives to it, in some sense, that quality which will not pass away. This love is an objective artifact in the spiritual realm and thus invests the object itself with a new kind of objectivity that it lacks by virtue of its mere existence. Consider as a concrete example of this effect how the second and third class relics of saints have objective spiritual power which endures in the material world.

Avarice is a perversion of this relationship. A person in the grip of this vice seeks to secure his own value through goods. He becomes "attached," that is, instead of assimilating objects into his own identity in order to instill genuine value in them, he attempts to assimilate his identity into the objects of his possession. The perpetual grasping after more and more objects is merely the outward manifestation of this interior spiritual transaction. No goods are ever sufficient to underwrite the identity of a person, because the value of goods comes from the person in the first place. The avaricious man, instead of taking pleasure in his goods — that is, instead of taking the pleasure which he has in his soul and allowing it to manifest as pleasure in the good things around him — hopes that the goods themselves will be able to provide him with pleasure. However, because goods are only able to express the value that the person has put into them, no amount of multiplication will ever bring a man more joy than he has to impart. The multiplication of desires is a frantic casting about for more value by the man who has material excess coupled with interior privation.

This means that the foundation of all values, including the value that a person finds in exterior material goods, is interior self-possession. The "genuine riches" of which Christ speaks are the spiritual currency that is able to invest value in exterior things. A person who has the spirit of poverty is not one who denies himself the good things of the earth but rather one who is able to gain more enjoyment from a very small number of earthly things than other men are able to gain from oceans of wealth. By increasing his spiritual capital, the virtuous man is enabled to impart more value to the things around him, to love them more and in a more ordered way. He therefore becomes particular about investing his wealth, and assigns value only to those things which will bring him a good return in the spiritual realm — in the same way that a shrewd businessman does not play the lottery, the virtuous man does not throw away his love on baubles. He wisely chooses only those objects which will assist him in attaining his spiritual goals.

LAUNDERED MONEY

Give and there will be gifts for you: a full measure, pressed down, shaken together, and running over, will be poured into your lap; because the amount you measure out is the amount you will be given back.

Luke 6:38

When goods are exchanged for money, they lose a part of their value. If goods are given as gifts, they not only retain their value, they increase it. In the transmission from gift-giver to gift-receiver, the object takes on an added value: it becomes a sign of the relationship that exists between the two parties. The original form of the gift is perfect reciprocity: Adam receives Eve, and Eve in return receives Adam. The exchange of selves, consummated in sexuality, is mutual and simultaneous. Gift exchange makes it possible to image this self-giving in the world of material things, which is why Lewis Hyde refers to gift exchange as the "erotic life of property."

There are several different senses in which we speak of gifts, but "common to each of them is the notion that a gift is a thing we do not get by our own efforts. We cannot buy it; we cannot acquire it through an act of will. It is bestowed on us." Hyde also notes that "a cardinal property of the gift [is that] whatever we have been given is supposed to be given away again, not kept." Either the gift itself, or something of equal value, is to be passed along to the next person in the chain. This is a counter-intuitive statement for most people in Western civilization. We tend to think of private property as primary in a way that occludes the universal destination of goods; a gift becomes a possession as soon as it is received.

If we look at the original gifts, however, it is clear that the circulation and transmission of gifts is essential to their nature. All human life is derived from the peculiar form of gift-exchange that we call sex. The man gives himself to the woman, and the woman to the man, but their self-giving only achieves its full purpose when it allows them to transmit the gift of self to a new person: literally, in giving themselves to one another, they give selfhood to a new human being. It is not by accident that a culture which conceives of gift exchange as a closed as opposed to circular transaction is also a culture which contracepts and aborts.

The greatest gift ever given also affirms this principle of the transmission of gifts. Christ came down from Heaven in order to assume a human body. He received the body as a gift from Mary, who had in turn received it as a gift from the Holy Spirit. He gave that body up as a gift for the salvation of all mankind, and established a perpetual cycle of gift exchange which we reenact at every Mass. The faithful receive the Body and Blood of Christ, they are sent out into the world to "love and serve the Lord," and then they return the next week to make a gift to God of all that they have done, loving and serving Him in the intervening days. This gift, the Offertory, is received by God under the symbols of bread and wine, the "work of human hands," and the gift is recirculated once more as the Body and Blood of Christ.

This gift of the Body and Blood of Christ is the gift of identity: the communicant is not only receiving his God at the moment of communion, he is also receiving himself. He is sent out into the world bearing his own identity as an adopted son of God. While he is in the world, he is expected to invest this gift in good works so that, like the good and faithful servants in the parable of the talents (see Mark 25:14-30), when he returns and once more offers himself to God, what he

30

offers has been enriched. This enriched personal identity is incorporated into the Church, the Body of Christ, and returned to the communicant once more, again enriched by the gifts which all of the other faithful have brought to the Offertory since he last received. Slowly, through this process, all things are reconciled in Christ, who makes them new.

Given that gift exchange is such a powerful symbol, it is easy to imagine it as an exclusively positive transaction, and to glorify gift economies over market economies. It is important to keep in mind, however, that the best things are always open to perversion: just as sexuality becomes destructive if it is not mutual, open and reciprocal, gift exchange becomes negative, even poisonous, if it is used improperly.

A gift should express the personality of the giver, and their appreciation for the needs or desires of the one who receives. "Thoughtless" gifts, that is, gifts which have no personal dimension, are often harmful if they are given in the context of a relationship that should be intimate. Gifts that are bought with money tend to lose their meaning and significance unless they are fortified with time and effort, or they address a pressing need on the part of the recipient or represent an amount of money that would be a significant sacrifice for the giver.

Gifts may also become perverse if they are used as a means of producing obligation or exacting gratitude. Women especially are prone to giving gifts in order to guilt-trip the recipient into giving them back something that they want, or in order to build up a reserve of obligatory gratitude which they can leverage into moral power and authority. Gifts of this sort are often called "white elephants," because these animals were once given as poisoned presents in India: it was superficially an honor to own one because they were sacred, but it was in fact a real pain in the ass because you weren't allowed to corral the sacred beast and had to let it rampage freely around your gardens. Receiving gifts of this kind is unpleasant, but turning them down is difficult because the giver is attached to the return that they expect to receive on their gift. Reciprocity, good-will and authenticity are necessary to ensure the integrity of gift exchange.

VOLUNTARY SIMPLICITY

How happy are the poor in spirit; theirs is the kingdom of heaven.

Matthew 5:3

Once upon a time, a man who had two blankets, and a tent of his own, and enough meat to get him through the winter was rich. Today, a man who has only two blankets, nothing but a tent to live in, and just enough meat to get him through the winter is considered extremely poor. The rich man in the tent never thought of himself as poor. He didn't look with envy on other men and didn't feel the stigmatization of being of the lowest class. He didn't think, "Look at me, I have not a computer, or electric heating, or running water, or many delicacies for the table. Woe. Alas. For I have been born into a century of poverty and privation."

Most of the suffering associated with poverty is the suffering of feeling poor and the fear of being treated like a poor person. People tend to stereotype those who are beneath them on the social ladder as stupid, lazy, and uncouth. The rich habitually treat the poor as second class citizens and have done so since Scriptural times. "The proud man thinks humility abhorrent; so too, the rich abominate the poor" (Ecclus 13:20).

Judgments of this sort are traditionally based on class distinctions. We tend to think that these distinctions no longer exist in "the land of equal opportunity," but this is only because these distinctions are now tacitly understood and silently maintained. For example, most municipal planners take the trouble to ensure that people living in cities are stratified according to class. Zoning bylaws are used to control and corral poverty, but it is not just that the poor are ghettoized. The middle class, and even the rich, are also pushed into isolated ghettos where they are functionally prevented from having access to the wider range of social conditions that exist within the same metropolitan sphere — often within blocks of one another. This is good for commerce because it deprives people of a sense of perspective and wards off the danger of pricked consciences and social responsibility. The rich man will always find it much easier to ignore Lazarus if, instead of languishing on his doorstep, Lazarus is politely shoved into an out-of-the-way slum where the rich man need not see him.

The segregation of the classes creates the illusion of poverty within spheres of affluence. People tend to have the most contempt for those who are only one or two rungs below them on the social ladder, whereas they feel pity for those who live further down. This creates intense personal anxiety about any diminution of one's social status.

The cure for this insular obsession with keeping up appearances is solidarity. Solidarity is very different from pity. When rich Westerners wring their hands about the plight of war orphans, that is pity. When rich Westerners fly to war-torn countries and put their bodies in the way of the guns, knowing that people will wake up and pay attention if an American citizen gets shot, that's solidarity. It means entering into other people's suffering in order to have a genuine understanding of what their experience is like, and it means making use of one's wealth and of the status and influence associated with wealth to improve the conditions of the less fortunate.

Gandhi did this. He traveled all over India by train, riding third class. By riding with poor people, he learned about their lives and gained a real experience of what it was like to suffer the privations that they were suffering. He concluded that "the people in high places...who generally travel in superior classes, [should] without previous warning, go through the experiences now and then of third class traveling. We would then soon see a remarkable change in the conditions of third class traveling and the uncomplaining millions will get some return for the fares they pay under the expectation of being carried from place to place with ordinary creature comforts."

Those who have actually lived with the poor and shared their poverty do not feel pity. This is because the actual experience of suffering bears almost no relationship to the imaginary experience of suffering: the idea of poverty is much harder to bear than actual poverty. When we look upon "the tragic spectacle of misery and poverty that people tend to ignore in order to salve their consciences" (*Populorum Progressio*), what we feel is guilt. Pity is not a form of compassion, but a form of self-accusation. The burning in the heart, the tears welling up in the eyes, the sinking feeling in the gut when you look at an image of a starving child is in no way similar to the hunger and desperation that the child feels. If you get people from your parish to sponsor you to go to Africa and suffer in solidarity with that child, you won't feel anything that is even remotely the same as what you feel when watching the World Vision commercials.

"In economic matters, respect for human dignity requires the practice of...*solidarity,* in accordance with the golden rule and in keeping with the generosity of the Lord, who 'though he was rich, yet for your sake...became poor so that by his poverty, you might become rich'" (CCC 2407).

Solidarity creates a sense of perspective. Poverty voluntarily accepted is not that difficult to bear. Even if you are cold and hungry, you still have all of your faculties, and all of the good things of the earth to cheer you. If you have experienced this, it makes it a lot harder to get really worked up about trifling privations. This perspective does not, however, lead to carelessness towards others. In times of plenty, we tend to get relatively little out of our riches: the thought of losing them makes us anxious, but the fact of owning them gives little joy. Those who have practiced solidarity understand how the poor feel about receiving the things that they have been hoping and praying for. Instead of giving out of a sense of guilt or pity, they give because they realize how much more joy the poor could be getting out of their wealth than they are getting out of it themselves.

INVOLUNTARY SIMPLICITY

It is a question of balancing what happens to be your surplus now against their present need, and one day they may have something to spare that will supply your own need. That is how we strike a balance: as scripture says: The man who gathered much had none too much, the man who gathered little did not go short.

2 Corinthians 8:13-15

When St. Paul called upon the people of Corinth to give generously to the collection for the needs of the Church, he referred to their wealth as "your surplus now." Corinth was a wealthy town, and the Corinthians could reasonably expect to go on being affluent for many years to come. Yet Saint Paul seems to appreciate the point made by the author of Ecclesiastes: "There is a season for everything" (3:1). Riches will come, and riches will go. Poverty will rise, and poverty will end. There is no security in the pursuit of wealth, "for it is able to sprout wings like an eagle that flies off to the sky" (Prov 23:5).

The obvious solution to the problem of the insecurity of riches is to build up savings during times of plenty, so that you will have something to live on during times of poverty. This is not, however, the solution which Christ proposes. Having called the industrious man who saves his wealth for the future a "fool" in the twelfth chapter of Luke, He goes on to praise a crafty and dishonest steward in the sixteenth.

There was a rich man and he had a steward who was denounced to him for being wasteful with his property. He called for the man and said, "What is this I hear about you? Draw me up an account of your stewardship because you are not to be my steward any longer." Then the steward said to himself, "Now that my master is taking the stewardship from me, what am I to do? Dig? I am not strong enough. Go begging? I should be too ashamed. Ah, I know what I will do to make sure that when I am dismissed from office there will be some to welcome me into their homes."

Then he called his master's debtors one by one. To the first he said, "How much do you owe my master?" "One hundred measures of oil" was the reply. The steward said, "Here, take your bond; sit down straight away and write fifty." To another he said, "And you, sir, how much do you owe?" "One hundred measures of wheat" was the reply. The steward said, "Here, take your bond and write eighty."

The master praised the dishonest steward for his astuteness. For the children of this world are more astute in dealing with their own kind than are the children of light.

And so I tell you this: use money, tainted as it is, to win you friends, and thus make sure that when it fails you, they will welcome you into the tents of eternity. (Luke 16:1-9)

This is a very bizarre parable. It's difficult to imagine the master that Christ portrays: clearly the man is angry at the beginning with the steward's mismanagement of his affairs, and yet at the end he praises the steward for his further misconduct. What could this mean?

Let's analyze the parable as an allegory for the relationship between men and God. Every man is a steward of the wealth of the earth, of his own time, and of his own soul

— and all are guilty of mismanagement. We all know that sooner or later God is going to ask for an accounting of our stewardship and that we are going to come up short. So what ought we to do?

The steward in Christ's parable has been given charge of the master's material wealth, and he has been responsible for contracting various debts with people in the community. Notice that the steward does not cook the books in order to embezzle funds for himself, but rather cooks them in favor of his neighbors. In the world, it would be dishonest for the steward to forgive these debts, but in the spiritual life, it is good, indeed praiseworthy, to forgive the debts of others. The steward is astute because he recognizes what many Christians have not noticed: that friendships and fraternity with other men is of greater value than wealth. The steward is going to lose control of the master's wealth — it is perishable, and it is to be taken from him; his friendships, however, he will retain, and his friends will "welcome him into the tents of eternity."

The wisdom of the world says that you should never lend money to your friends because it will cause resentment and discomfort when they fail to repay you. Christ says exactly the opposite. You ought to lend money to your friends, especially when you have no reasonable expectation that they will repay. In fact, if they're unlikely ever to repay you, all the better. Resentment and discomfort only arise if you have your heart set on getting back what you have given. If you lend money and don't worry about getting it back, there is no problem: you may get the money back at some unexpected date, as Saint Paul suggests, or you may reap a harvest of increased friendship and gratitude, as Christ tells us. Either way, sooner or later you are going to need something. It might be money, or it might be something more valuable than money, but if you give your surplus away now, then the things you need will be there when you need them.

The more that a man invests in cementing relationships and supporting the least of God's people, the greater a return he will gain — either when calamity strikes him, or when he arrives before the throne of God and is asked for an account of his life.

MUCH ADO

Three-fourths of the demands existing in the world are romantic: founded on visions, idealisms, hopes, and affections; and the regulation of the purse is, in its essence, regulation of the imagination and the heart.... We need examples of people who, leaving to Heaven to decide whether they are to rise in the world, decide for themselves that they will be happy in it, and have resolved to seek — not greater wealth, but simpler pleasure, not higher fortune, but deeper felicity; making the first of possessions, self-possession.

John Ruskin

Buddha's most famous saying is that "the root of all suffering is desire." This is one of those truths that perennially pops up in the writings of sages, but which seems very counterintuitive to non-sages. Okay, let's say that I am in intense physical pain. I am suffering. How does my suffering have anything to do with desire?

The person who is suffering from physical pain is suffering primarily from the desire not to be in pain. The athlete who pushes himself to the very limit of physical endurance, who can feel his sinews protesting, his lungs aching, his muscles straining, and his entire body crying out for relief — he does not suffer. He has chosen this pain, and he thinks that it is good. He may even come to desire the pain because he associates it with victory and self-mastery. The same might be said of a woman in childbirth: if she chooses to think of the pain as a helper in the process of giving life, as a sign that her body is doing what it is supposed to be doing, and as a means of becoming united to the Cross of Christ,

41

then she doesn't suffer. She's still in pain, but pain and suffering are two distinct phenomena, and the relationship between them is not absolute.

The trouble with Buddha's dictum is that in both of these cases the natural desire to avoid pain is put aside for the sake of another, stronger desire: the desire for athletic accomplishment or the desire for a child to be born. The athlete risks defeat, and the woman risks stillbirth. This is why Buddhism itself is so difficult: in order to attain perfect Enlightenment, it is not only necessary to overcome every other form of desire for the sake of Enlightenment, it is also necessary to overcome the desire for Enlightenment itself. Fortunately, we are Christians. We need not worry about the paradoxes of Nirvana, because Christianity believes both in ordered desires and in legitimate sufferings.

What Christianity tries to do away with are disordered desires and the needless sufferings that they breed. Contemporary culture is inimical to this goal because people who have self-possession and inner tranquility do not make good consumers. Consumer capitalism relies on the multiplication of desires and on the maintenance of a constant state of mild suffering. Advertising constantly confronts the viewer with the spectacle of immaterial goods which he wants but does not possess. Desires for family, love, freedom, beauty, peace, rest, joy, sexual attraction, accomplishment, praise and even a unique personal identity are all awakened by advertising. The ad then promises that the product which it is flogging will fulfill the spiritual longing that it has just awakened.

What effect does this have on the culture? If I go out in search of my true inner self, and I have been conditioned to believe that I can achieve a unique personality by choosing one of six customized cellphones, then I might go and buy a cell phone in order to make myself feel unique. But hold! I soon notice that other people are sporting the same cellphone;

my unique identity is also their unique identity. I have been duped. So now what do I do? Clearly I must go and seek out another good which will do what the cell-phone did not. Since all of this occurs on a subconscious level, I never have the opportunity to sit the advertisement down and question it about its broken promises, nor does it occur to me that perhaps there is nothing for sale anywhere, in any market, no matter how far off the beaten track, that will give me the identity that I crave.

Eventually, when I have made enough attempts to buy my Self on the free market, I despair. I no longer think that a unique personality is something that exists: all human beings are just personas, a collection of scripts and memes learned from television and society. It's just a matter of finding a niche where you can comfortably fit in and live in repressed desperation for the rest of your life. It is not, I think, by accident that a society which is constantly proclaiming that love, God, beauty, and joy are on sale at Walmart is also a society which has lost faith in love, God, beauty, and joy.

Detachment from material things begins with the recognition that people need the spiritual goods which they are trying to get by buying things, and proceeds to the acknowledgment that these goods are attainable only through the cultivation of virtue. This involves turning off the tap: so long as it looks like there might be another, easier way, human nature will pursue the wide road to disappointment and jaded ironicism. If the desire for material goods is constantly piqued by advertising and constantly placated by buying, the intellectual knowledge that material goods never truly satisfy will never amount to anything more than a lofty and impractical ideal. The unconscious self will go right on consuming, hoping, being dissatisfied, and consuming again.

The attainment of virtue, and therefore of happiness, depends on interior freedom from compulsive desires. In order to attain that freedom, it is necessary to starve out the desires. Most people tend to think that this means a loss of pleasure, but that is absolutely untrue. Interior freedom begins with the denial of disordered pleasures, not because pleasure is bad, but because disordered pleasure is too transient and reductive.

People underestimate the pleasures of self-mastery because they are unfamiliar with them. It is easy to prove, however, that enslavement to desire is undesirable. No sane person ever seeks to have an inordinate desire that he does not have already. A man who is naturally temperate will not sit around thinking, "Ah, if only it were my habit to arise each morning unsure of my surroundings, to guzzle twelve pints of 'eavy before luncheon, and to spend my evenings invoking Ralph and Huey before the porcelain altar!" A person without vainglorious pride never muses, "Why do people like me? Why does no one curse or revile me? If only I could be reckoned an arrogant buffoon!" No one who is untroubled by lust thinks, "Oh my soul! Where are your venereal diseases? Whence thine erectile dysfunction?" Unless already in the grip of an excessive drive one does not actively desire to be its slave.

OVER TIME

The supply of time is truly a daily miracle, an affair genuinely astonishing when one examines it. You wake up in the morning, and lo! your purse is magically filled with twenty-four hours of the unmanufactured tissue of the universe of your life! It is yours. It is the most precious of possessions. A highly singular commodity, showered upon you in a manner as singular as the commodity itself!

Arnold Bennet

Money is time. Every dollar that a person earns is a representation of the time that it took him to earn it. Money can be multiplied almost endlessly, but time is limited — and of the two it is by far the more valuable. The perennial desire of Pharaohs and emperors to somehow convert their gold into eternal life is a blaring acknowledgment of this fact; they entomb themselves amidst their treasures and lie in silence, waiting for more time. A man arriving at the end of his life would happily give away everything that he owns for another hour, another day, another week of life. Money can only buy stuff; time buys existence. This is why the business adage that "time is money" is backwards: it assumes that money is the thing that you want, and time is the worthless stuff that you are going to convert into it.

Time is also the currency of identity. Whatever a person does with his time is what he becomes. Personalities are developed by expending time: What makes a man charming? That he has spent time learning droll phrases and has practiced deploying them in his speech. What makes a girl intelligent? That she has employed herself in the reading of books and the thinking of lofty thoughts. Natural talent affords only a small advantage and will amount to nothing if it is not developed through the expenditure of time.

All time is not, however, equal. Peter Kreeft points out that there are two different kinds of time, and uses the Greek words *chronos* and *kairos* to distinguish them. *Chronos* is time that can be measured. It is a dimension of the physical universe, and we can mostly behave as though it is fixed and constant. *Kairos* is fluid time, life time, the sort of time that we are speaking of when we say, "time flies when you're having fun," or when we try to come up with ways of "making the time pass more quickly." It is time as perceived by a human mind. Each man receives each day an equal allotment of *chronos*, which he may then convert into as much or as little *kairos* as he chooses.

Chronos becomes *kairos* through the application of consciousness. When the will claims a piece of time, it fashions and shapes it, invests it with meaning (the "fullness" of time), or destroys it (killing time). The shape of a moment, a day, or a life is determined by the way in which a person chooses to interact with time.

These interactions are formed through the practice of "presence" or of "absence." Sometimes we speak of a person as being "absent" from the room that they are in: this is not necessarily an indication that that person has ceased to be present to time, but it does mean that they have ceased to be present in space. Their body remains, but the mind has gone wandering off and has divorced itself from its physical surroundings. The same effect takes place in time. The mind shuts out the world and stops paying attention as time dribbles by. Routines and habits often have this effect. People who feel that their lives are draining away are generally those who have learned to go through much of their day on autopilot; they have ceased to be present to themselves in time.

Reclaiming lost time involves choosing to be present. Certain types of thoughts, feelings, daydreams, and activities kill time because they don't engage the will. For an example, let us turn to the dead horse of bad American television. This is the classic example of "wasting time," but there's really no reason why time spent watching TV has to be wasted. A person could watch the same show over and over again and still choose to claim something new out of the experience on each occasion: They could analyze the dialogue in order to make a study of speech patterns. They could learn to imitate the different characters to amuse their friends at parties. They could observe how the emotional content of the show is altered by different commercials playing during the breaks. They could dissect the program to learn about the structure of narrative. They could take in the vision expressed through lighting and color choices and practice seeing the real world around them as though it had been shot in that way. The most banal material, introduced into the human mind, becomes a bit of media that can be molded by creativity and intelligence into a thousand different psychological, spiritual, and intellectual products. Or it can be allowed to wash over the mind as an indifferent haze, producing nothing.

Kairos can also be multiplied through judicious use of multitasking. Imprudent multitasking tends to produce interior disorientation and overload, resulting in a loss of time. Instead of paying attention to four or five different things at once, the mind becomes so divided that it is not really paying attention to any of them, and true presence of mind is lost. Some activities, however, can be effectively conjoined. Many simple physical tasks, such as washing dishes or stuffing envelopes, leave the mind free to wander. Generally, the mind will do just that: meander aimlessly through a series of worries, daydreams, half-formed thoughts, and vague imaginings. These thoughts are so insipid that they cannot be recalled afterwards and bear no fruit. It is possible to reclaim this lost thought-time by willfully harnessing it to a particular purpose: prayer, philosophy, development of inspirations, problem solving, invention, and other mental tasks.

Just as God has given the earth to us in order to cultivate it and make it bring forth fruit, so too has He given us time. Thoreau observed that you cannot "kill time without injuring eternity." Eternity is not, as many imagine, an empty timelessness. The New Heaven and the New Earth will not be a permanent homeostatic universe in which the blessed sit in a state of absolute rest contemplating the unmoving God. This vision is uninspiring because it is dead. It suggests that eternity itself is the killer of time — not merely the end of *chronos*, but the death of *kairos*. Such an eternity could never be the habitation of the living God.

We ought instead to imagine eternity as the consummation of time, the reconciliation of all history into a perfect and organic unity. God does not experience no-time, but rather all-time, a perfect simultaneity in which all of the riches of time are absolutely and eternally present. When human beings work and cultivate the time that is given to them, they enrich their identities, which are then incorporated into Christ through the mystery of the Church. When it is actively employed to develop personality, time is enabled to bring forth fruit which will endure into eternity.

BUY NOTHING

Here is a man whose desires are few. In some things he will not be able to maintain his resolution but they will be few. Here is a man whose desires are many. In some things he will be able to maintain his resolution but they will be few.

Confucius

God demands a tithe of time. Material goods, if allowed to do so, will consume a person's life. They take time to produce, and they take time to maintain. Things establish a hold on human life through covetousness. Even before the thing is acquired, the desire for ownership demands an expenditure of thought and energy. Once goods are obtained man becomes in a sense a servomechanism of his possessions.

The need to preserve time from the tyranny of commodities used to be e by the Sabbath rest. God wisely instructed His people to put aside one day out of every seven to do nothing. This rest was a cease from toil and also a cease from buying and selling. "Remember the Sabbath day and keep it holy. For six days you shall labor and do all your work, but the seventh day is a Sabbath for Yahweh your God. You shall do no work that day, neither you nor your son nor your daughter nor your servants, men or women, nor your animals nor the stranger who lives with you. For in six days Yahweh made the heavens and the earth and the sea and all that these hold, but on the seventh day he rested; that is why Yahweh has blessed the Sabbath day and made it sacred" (Exod 20:9-11).

It's worth noting that God is not just instructing people to rest for their own sake. Half of the text is devoted to

49

making it clear that the injunction to rest is absolute: it's not just so that the rich can have a nice day off to go picnicking with their families. It's also so that the laborers, the slaves, and even the cattle can have some time of their own. It is not a coincidence that the abandonment of this commandment in the modern world has gone hand-in-hand with the exploitation of laborers and the loss of real leisure amongst the lower classes.

The prohibition on forcing others to work is also a commandment to release oneself from bondage to things. When the Mosaic law was given, people's primary possessions were their land, their slaves, and their cattle. Moses commanded them to spend an entire day every week in freedom from their goods: their slaves and their cattle would have rest, and they also would have rest from the responsibility of stewarding. This legislation of freedom from material concerns also extended to the land: obviously the land itself could not take a day off. Sun would continue to shine, and the corn would continue to ripen in the fields. Therefore, a sabbatical year was also commanded: "For six years you may sow your land and gather its produce, but in the seventh year you must let it lie fallow and forgo all produce from it" (Exod 23:10-11).

The Sabbath encouraged detachment from temporal goods by putting aside a tithe of time for God. "You must keep the Sabbaths carefully because the Sabbath is a sign between myself and you from generation to generation to show that it is I, Yahweh, who sanctify you" (Exod 31:13). One of the great, perennial temptations is the inclination to found personal worth and identity in money and in the acquisition of material goods. The Sabbath, by forcing people to take an entire day every week to stop working and trading, forced them to look within, to confront themselves in relation to God, and to firmly establish the parts of the self that are not related to ownership.

Few people, even today, would openly admit to themselves that their sense of self-worth is based on their money, but it is experimentally demonstrable. Left-wing activists have tried to institute a sort of secular Sabbath, a day of rest that comes around not once a week but once a year. It is called "Buy Nothing Day." Very few people participate, and many of those who do find it tremendously difficult. This is very revealing: it means that socially conscious lefties who are ideologically committed to disentangling themselves from the mechanisms of consumer culture are addicted to shopping — so addicted that it seems like a serious mortification to forgo spending money for a single day out of the year. If you are inclined to jump on your high horse and start opining about how a life divorced from God is sure to produce such perversions, stop and think again: many of the socially conscious lefties in question are Christians sporting "What Would Jesus Buy" t-shirts.

The link between identity and shopping is revealed by the sense of boredom that prompts people to shop and that arises very quickly if the ability to shop is withheld. Recall that time is the currency of identity: if most of a person's time is spent earning money to buy goods, shopping for goods, watching television whose primary purpose is to flog goods, and using or maintaining the goods that they own, the result is going to be an identity that is very closely bound to commercial life. If that person stops buying and selling, the result is a deep and unreasonable sense of angst. At exactly what point this will kick in is different from person to person: some people become anxious if they find themselves in a place where the stores are not open twenty-four hours per day, others will get antsy halfway through Buy Nothing Day, and others will start to get the shakes after a week of consumer detox. The sense of boredom — of "not knowing what to do" with oneself — is a profound indication that there is a hole in one's personal identity that is being filled by the consumption of goods.

When goods are filling in for deeper personal needs, the relationship with them becomes compulsive. Most people will only apply the term "shopaholic" to someone who is more addicted to shopping than they are, yet anyone who can't easily go one day a week without shopping is clearly an addict. Addicts are not free to make rational choices about what they will and will not consume. They are not able to spend their money responsibly, and they are not capable of practicing meaningful detachment from the objects of their addiction.

Detachment from consumer addiction is not an optional adjunct to the spiritual life. The practice of constant production and constant consumption is a real, objective evil. God was not joking around when He instituted mandatory rest: the first man who ever got caught gathering wood on the Sabbath was taken out of the camp and stoned to death. 24/7 consumerism exhausts the least of our brothers who are forced to toil without ceasing; it exhausts the earth, which is never allowed to recover from our constant demands on its resources; and it exhausts the interior resources of the self, which are never refreshed at the springs of silence and contemplation.

SELL EVERYTHING

Why are you so sick at heart, when you hear the words, "Sell your possessions"? For if, on the one hand, these possessions could follow you into the afterlife, they should not therefore be highly valued, when next to the prizes that await there they should be thrown into the shade.

Saint Basil the Great

Material goods really are good. There's nothing wrong with riches, only with attachment to riches. "You must not love this passing world or anything that is in the world. The love of the Father cannot be in any man who loves the world, because nothing the world has to offer — the sensual body, the lustful eye, pride in possessions — could ever come from the Father but only from the world" (1 John 2:15-16). Notice that Christ defines the "world" in terms of concupiscence: it is not the body, but the sensual body, not the eye, but the lustful eye, not possessions, but the pride in them that prevents a man from having the love of the Father.

For those who have taken vows of religious poverty, it is theoretically very simple to give up the attachment to worldly things. Simple — not easy. To paraphrase the American military's ninth principle of warfare, "Everything in the spiritual life is simple, but the simple thing is difficult." It would seem that the problem is less simple when there is a family involved. Parents cannot simply eschew wealth: they must have enough goods to provide for their children, and they must responsibly manage these goods in the hopes of keeping the family from falling into squalor and want.

It's very tempting to think that these responsibilities soften Christ's teachings about money. After all, it's not possible or morally responsible for a father to follow Jesus' advice to "go and sell what you own and give the money to the poor, and you will have treasure in heaven; then come, follow me" (Matt 19:21-22). Or is it?

St. Paul makes an interesting point: people should provide first for their family and for their friends, because if someone you love is in need it is less humiliating for them to receive from you than for them to go out begging. A parent is someone who has in their house a number of very poor people. Children do not have wealth. They don't earn money. They exist in a state of natural mendicancy. A parent holds certain goods in trust for their children; just as you can't rob from the poor to give to the poor, you can't sell the things that your kids need in order to give them to others. This does not contradict Christ's saying about selling everything.

It also does not mean, however, that parents can justify a life of luxury and excess simply on the basis that they need to buy things for their children. Detachment from temporal goods is essential to family life — just as essential as it is to religious life. The Pontifical Council for the Family points out that "Parents must trustingly and courageously train their children in the essential values of human life. Children must grow up with a correct attitude of freedom with regard to material goods, by adopting a simple and austere lifestyle and being fully convinced that man is more precious for what he is than for what he has." Children learn how to interact with material goods by watching their parents. A child's demands not only can be refused, they must be refused if the child is ever going to learn self-control, patience, or moderation. Parents who are not, themselves, detached from riches are doing their children a disservice if they use their parenthood to justify passing the addiction to stuff on to the next generation.

Many parents feel frustrated and even enslaved by the constant demands of their children for more and more things. These demands arise because the children are accustomed to getting what they want and because they have modeled their own relationship with material goods on the example set by their parents. In many families, serious conflicts arise because the parents do not moderate their children's desires. The mother feels lonely and undersupported by the father, and in order to alleviate her frustrations she goes shopping. The husband feels pressured to earn more money in order to keep up with the financial demands of his wife, and as a consequence he overworks himself and is unable to be emotionally available to his family. If the issue comes to a head, the woman will claim that she is only spending money to buy the things that the children need, and the man will say he can only work so many hours a week. Thus the cycle is perpetuated.

Children who grow up in such households come to be addicted to material goods and simultaneously to resent the goods given to them by their parents. Fathers who have spent their entire lives working to provide good things for their children, but who have defined "good things" primarily in terms of material goods, are often frustrated when their children reject them in adolescence and adulthood. This rejection is the result of a perception on the part of the children that they have been loved improperly: that their fathers didn't care enough to support the family spiritually and that they were trying to "buy love" by showering their children with material possessions.

Attachment to material goods also prevents parents from being generous in giving life. Many parents justify the decision to contracept or even to abort their children on the basis that if they had more, the existing children would be impoverished. They believe that their children would benefit more from being able to wear brand new clothing and have the latest video games than they would from having more siblings. This attitude on the part of the parents is inevitably passed along to their children, who come to believe that material goods are more important than human beings. This leads to enslavement to transitory pleasures and an inability to form real relationships later in life. Children who have not learned to have a proper respect for the dignity and primacy of the value of human life will inevitably lack a sense of their own value.

FLAT BROKE

I have learnt to manage on whatever I have, I know how to be poor and I know how to be rich too. I have been through my initiation and now I am ready for anything anywhere: full stomach or empty stomach, poverty or plenty.

Philippians 4:11-12

Poverty is relative. Most people living in America today, when asked to what class they belong, reply that they are middle class. People who earn twenty thousand dollars a year feel this, as do those who earn two hundred thousand dollars. Almost all people, regardless of class or income, feel that they are "just getting by" and that if they only had a little more income they would be able to live comfortably.

This feeling can be explained largely in terms of addiction to luxuries. People get accustomed to a certain standard of living and feel that their financial security is really threatened if they have to start cutting back: "it isn't for the sake of clothing or food that riches are a matter of such concern to so many people; but, by a certain wily artifice of the devil, countless pretexts of expenditure are proposed to the rich, so that they strive for superfluous, useless things as though they were necessary, and so that nothing measures up to their conception of what they should spend" (St. Basil the Great).

This lack of perspective is partly fueled by the expectation of constantly increasing prosperity. Young people generally expect that they will begin their independent adult lives at the level of wealth achieved by their parents and will continue to amass a greater fortune from that point onward.

Many take "entry-level" jobs assuming that they will earn promotions and become more wealthy over time. People then borrow against the anticipation of their future prosperity: they buy what they cannot afford today because they project a future in which they will be able to pay for it. Although people expect that over time their income will rise, they do not have a corresponding expectation that the cost of living will increase. The staggering amount of personal debt owed by Americans is the fruit of this shortsightedness.

Another reason that people overspend is that they have unrealistic perceptions of what constitutes a reasonable standard of living for someone in their income bracket. On television, young singles are consistently portrayed living in affluent neighborhoods, wearing expensive clothing and jewelry, and owning a wide variety of luxury goods. Although these characters work ordinary jobs, they are able to afford a standard of living that is vastly in excess of their income. Since many people today spend more time interacting with the people that they meet on TV than with real people in the world, they come to think that this is realistic, and as a result they feel anxious and dissatisfied with their own level of affluence.

It is for this reason that two of the Ten Commandments forbid covetousness. Covetousness is the interior state of mind that breeds unhappiness and dissatisfaction through comparison of oneself with others. These comparisons are fueled by judgments, which are expressed in the words that we choose to describe things. For example, if you choose to describe something as "low-class," "shabby," or "cheap," that will cause you to feel deprived if you are unable to afford anything better. When words like this are assigned to human beings, it creates a fear of being like those people. The choice to ascribe positive words like "sophisticated," "classy," or "elegant" to luxury objects and to affluent people, creates covetousness. One comes to feel that by owning the objects which are owned by higher class people, one will also come to possess a web of vaguely positive qualities which are associated with wealth.

Notice that the saints do not use these words. Christ refers to money as "tainted," and to poverty as "blessed." Riches are regularly associated with avarice, corruption, dishonesty, wastefulness, extravagance, and arrogance. Poverty, on the other hand, is lovingly associated with simplicity, child-likeness, trust in providence, generosity, innocence, humility and honesty.

Reality is really quite malleable to human choices; whether you see yourself as rich or poor, deprived or blessed, is largely a matter of the will. The words that we choose structure our thought and instruct the mind in how to value and envision the realities that it encounters. Detachment is largely a mental process. If you can imagine yourself living without something, you can live without it. The difficulty that people run into when they lose things that they're used to having is that they are unable to form a coherent picture of their own happiness without those things. It is this interior disposition, not exterior ownership, that enslaves the soul.

BROKE EVEN

Not to enable the poor to share in our goods is to steal from them and deprive them of life. The goods we possess are not ours, but theirs.

Saint John Chrysostom

Before we get ahead of ourselves, a small caveat. The danger in any theory that assigns a great deal of responsibility and freedom to the human person is that people will direct the theory outward instead of inward. Instead of cultivating cheerful indifference to his own poverty, a man will be tempted to practice callous indifference to the poverty of others. Christ points out that usually these are inversely related: the man who is always looking out for the splinter in his brother's eye is usually the one with the lumber conglomerate in his own.

Genuine detachment from material goods is not the same as contempt for material creation or for the needs of the body, including other people's bodies. The person who cultivates detachment does not do so just so that he can enjoy perfect self-possession and conceive of himself as a sort of spiritual athlete. The purpose of human life lies in the other: all spiritual, intellectual, physical, material, and artistic achievements only achieve the dignity of truly human acts when they are directed towards the good of another person. Detachment, therefore, is cultivated with a view to generosity.

This means that detachment is a moral responsibility. It's not optional. A man who is not detached from his goods is not free to give them away to others: he will do so only rarely, with great reluctance, and will massively inflate the value of whatever sacrifices he does manage to make. Instead of growing in holiness, his generosity will only result in self-congratulation and pride. "O new calamity! this strange passion. Where moth corrupteth not, nor thief breaketh through, vainglory scattereth. This is the moth of those treasures there; this the thief of our wealth in heaven; this steals away the riches that cannot be spoiled" (Saint John Chrysostom).

Failure to observe our obligations to the poor is a grave injustice, as is illustrated by the story of Lazarus and the rich man.

> There was a rich man who used to dress in purple and fine linen and feast magnificently every day. And at his gate there lay a poor man called Lazarus, covered with sores, who longed to fill himself with the scraps that fell from the rich man's table. Dogs even came and licked his sores. Now the poor man died and was carried away by the angels to the bosom of Abraham. The rich man also died and was buried.
>
> In his torment in Hades he looked up and saw Abraham a long way off with Lazarus in his bosom. So he cried out, "Father Abraham, pity me and send Lazarus to dip the tip of his finger in water and cool my tongue, for I am in agony in these flames." "My son," Abraham replied "remember that during your life good things came your way, just as bad things came the way of Lazarus. Now he is being comforted here while you are in agony. But that is not all: between us and you a great gulf has been fixed, to stop anyone, if he wanted to, crossing from our side to yours, and to stop any crossing from your side to ours." (Luke 16:19-26)

Please consider the fact that there is no evidence within the text that the rich man acquired his wealth by any kind of dishonesty or injustice. Abraham specifically

61

describes his affluence as a product of fortune: "good things came your way." The man no doubt felt that he had earned his wealth and that it was his right to enjoy it. Yet he is condemned to Hell: the rich man is guilty of a mortal sin, not on account of what he has done, but on account of what he has failed to do.

"Man should not consider his material possessions as his own, but as common to all, so as to share them without hesitation when others are in need" (Saint Thomas Aquinas). No matter how hard someone works, everything that he owns is taken from the gift that was originally bestowed on all mankind. "You are not making a gift of what is yours to the poor man, but you are giving him back what is his. You have been appropriating things that are meant to be for the common use of everyone. The earth belongs to everyone, not to the rich" (Saint Ambrose).

It follows from this obligation in justice that money ought to be given to the poor without strings attached. If a man owes money to someone, he does not first inquire as to how the money will be spent and then pay it back. The person to whom the money rightfully belongs has the right to spend it however they wish. If they misuse it, that is their business and their responsibility. "The almsgiver is a harbor for those in necessity: a harbor receives all who have encountered shipwreck, and frees them from danger; whether they are bad or good or whatever they are who are in danger, it escorts them into its own shelter. So you likewise, when you see on earth the man who has encountered the shipwreck of poverty, do not judge him, do not seek an account of his life, but free him from his misfortune. God has excused you from all officiousness and meddlesomeness.... A judge is one thing, an almsgiver is another" (St. John Chrysostom).

EASY MONEY

The more we strive to secure a common good corresponding to the real needs of our neighbors, the more effectively we love them.

Caritas in Veritate

The fire and brimstone having been dispatched, it's important to ask what we, as citizens of wealthy nations, can do to ensure that we don't end up on the wrong side of that great gulf. I'm aware that these are treacherous waters. A certain percentage of all American Catholics have joined up wholeheartedly with the Republican party. Others have accepted the economic conservativism that is dominant in fundamentalist Protestant circles. And still others are devoted to the notion of rational self-interest embodied in the liberal ideals on which America was founded. I've heard it argued that Vatican social teaching is just a bone that the Church throws to the liberals, and that any form of redistributive social justice is a violation of the sixth commandment. I've also encountered some ingenious arguments for ignoring social justice issues, like the complaint that a Catholic has to choose between voting for the pro-life Republicans and the pro-"social justice" Democrats — the obvious inference being that abortion is the most important issue, and perhaps the only issue, in electoral politics, and that federal elections are the only arena in which a Catholic might be expected to be involved in political life.

Taking the sensitivity of the issues into account, I'm going to lean heavily on authoritative quotations from the Magisterium. Catholics who do not accept the social teachings expressed in papal encyclicals and in the Catechism should be aware that they are in dissent against the legitimate teaching authority of the Church. There is no difference, in terms of obedience, between a liberal who uses sophisticated rationalizations to justify homosexuality and contraception, and a conservative who uses sophisticated rationalizations to justify practices and policies which encourage economic growth at the expense of human dignity.

"Every Christian is called to practice this charity, in a manner corresponding to his vocation and according to the degree of influence he wields in the *pólis*. This is the institutional path — we might also call it the political path — of charity, no less excellent and effective than the kind of charity which encounters the neighbor directly, outside the institutional mediation of the *pólis*" (*Caritas in Veritate*).

The Church does not presume to lay out a specific political doctrine or to promulgate a specific economic system. She does, however, make it clear that *"Political authority* has the right and duty to regulate the legitimate exercise of the right to ownership for the sake of the common good" (CCC 2406). The Catechism likens the responsibilities of citizens towards the state to the duties of children towards their parents: unless a child would violate his own conscience, he is supposed to be obedient to his parents, and unless a man would violate his conscience he is supposed to be obedient to the state. This includes the payment of taxes — even though those taxes will inevitably be used to fund immoral projects. Almost all states, throughout all of history, have been guilty of oppressing their citizens, enslaving their neighbors, killing innocent people, and other egregious misuses of civil authority. They have all used some of the money collected in taxes to pay to accomplish these evils. Yet when the Pharisees approached Christ and asked Him about paying their taxes, Christ told them that they were to pay. This wasn't because the Emperor Tiberius was a really moral and humane ruler or because imperial Rome was an especially just and virtuous state.

Although the Church is generally vague — outlining principles for economic justice rather than prescribing particular solutions, She does make it clear that our moral obligations include practices which require genuine self-sacrifice. Paul VI proposed that, "Each man must examine his conscience, which sounds a new call in our present times. Is he prepared to support, at his own expense, projects and undertakings designed to help the needy? Is he prepared to pay higher taxes so that public authorities may expand their efforts in the work of development? Is he prepared to pay more for imported goods, so that the foreign producer may make a fairer profit?" (*Populorum Progressio*). If our idea of economic justice is primarily concerned with securing the North American economy, with lowering the prices that we pay for our own goods, or with lowering our taxes, then we're pretty far off the mark.

That said, the primary interaction that a Catholic has with the socio-economic life of his nation is not at the ballot box, but in the office and at the mall. The "systems of sin" that John Paul II identifies with the Culture of Death are systems which are guided and maintained by human beings, through human choices. These include the choices that people make in their places of work, and especially the choices that we make as consumers. Every single person who participates in economic life votes for the kind of economy that he wants every time he opens his wallet.

The Vatican makes it clear that "man is the source, the center, and the purpose of all socio-economic life," and that "the fundamental purpose of...productivity must not be the mere multiplication of products. It must not be profit or domination. Rather, it must be the service of man, and indeed of the whole man" (*Gaudium et Spes*). Economic liberalism assumes that whatever results in the greatest profit will ultimately be for the best, because the overall prosperity of a nation will trickle down to the lowest classes. This view of economic life fails to account for the fact that monetary wealth is not the *summum bonum* of human life, or even of economic life. The Church does not analyze economics primarily in terms of GDP, or any other method of measuring productivity, because the product is secondary. "Human labor which is expended in the production and exchange of goods or in the performance of services is superior to the other elements of economic life. For the latter have only the nature of tools" (*Gaudium et Spes*). In other words, if laborers are treated badly in order to secure a greater prosperity, as measured in money, for the nation as a whole, this is unjust — even if the laborers share in the "trickle-down" effects of wealth. I'm not saying that they do. I'm just saying that even if trickle-down economics were true, it wouldn't matter.

Why? Because the mere multiplication of material goods is less important to human life than respect for the dignity of the person. There are homeless people who will not accept free lodging and food if it is given in a way that is condescending and humiliating, because they would rather retain their dignity, even at the cost of physical hunger and suffering. When people are mistreated, underpaid, exploited, and seen merely as a "human resource" instead of human persons, they suffer something which cannot be justified or compensated for with a paltry handful of silver.

HARD CASH

Now if the earth truly was created to provide man with the necessities of life and the tools for his own progress, it follows that every man has the right to glean what he needs from the earth.

Populorum Progressio

All are responsible for all. If we buy goods made on the other side of the world, the people on the other side of the world become our neighbors. This is why most of the recent Vatican social teaching is concerned with global economics. *Caritas in Veritate,* for example, gives little direct advice to the man in the pew, focusing instead on the obligations of rich nations and international bodies. Part of the reason for this is that the obligations of individuals have been amply covered elsewhere: in the earlier social encyclicals, in the Catechism, and in Scripture itself.

Individual neglect of the poor is a serious sin. It is clear from the story of Lazarus and the rich man that it is possible to sin mortally by omission, and many of the most frightening passages in the gospel involve the damnation of people who firmly believed that they were doing the will of God. The primary reason which Matthew gives for the damnation of these souls is neglect of social obligations: "Go away from me, with your curse upon you, to the eternal fire prepared for the devil and his angels. For I was hungry and you never gave me food; I was thirsty and you never gave me anything to drink; I was a stranger and you never made me welcome, naked and you never clothed me, sick and in prison and you never visited me" (Matt 25:41-43).

Everyone has the right to work and benefit from the fruits of the earth. "Man's needs do not die out, but forever recur; although satisfied today, they demand fresh supplies for tomorrow. Nature accordingly must have given to man a source that is stable and remaining always with him, from which he might look to draw continual supplies. And this stable condition of things he finds solely in the earth and its fruits" (*Rerum Novarum*). Many of the economic practices by which the developed world gains the wealth of consumer goods that you and I purchase deprive people in poorer countries of the right or ability to profit from the natural resources of their own nations. For example, the excessive demand for textiles in North America results in arable land being used to grow cotton for Western consumption in areas of the world where people are starving to death because there is not enough food. A greater profit can be made selling cash crops to the West, than can be made feeding the local population, and many of these countries are so badly in debt that they have no choice but to starve their people in order to make their payments. The UN then declares that the world is "overpopulated" and proposes to abort the children of these people. Men are literally starving, and children being torn from their mothers' wombs, so that we can have our ribbons and bows.

It must be admitted that there is no simple solution for the Western consumer: there is no clear catalog of simple acts to avoid. Even people who are extremely conscientious about their social responsibilities often complain that no matter how hard they try, they keep discovering that the things which they consume have been produced under unjust and exploitative conditions. For this reason, people who like to keep their spirituality clean and legalistic tend to get frustrated with social justice issues.

There is no legalistic way of loving the poor. Personal responsibility for macroeconomics must be founded not on the avoidance of clearly outlined sins but on the cultivation of the virtues of generosity, frugality, and solidarity. There are plenty of excuses that get made for why we should go on consuming. Many argue that even if people who work for sixty cents an hour are not being paid a reasonable wage, it's better than having no job at all. This sort of logic allows injustices to multiply under the delusion that somehow by condoning evils it is possible to do good. Macroeconomic systems are made up of human choices: if the consumer is only concerned with getting the best price for himself and with amassing the most goods for his dollar, then the system will be concerned with the same things. Let's call this "trickle-up" economics: virtue practiced on the level of household finances and personal consumption will inevitably drive just practices on a global scale.

Overconsumption within the rich countries of the world necessitates the seizure of lands and resources from the poor. This seizure may be accomplished through violence, through economic domination, or through political maneuvering, but no matter how it is done, the result is the same. The poor are deprived of the ability to work the land on which they live. They are denied the right to be the first to profit from the fruits of the earth over which they labor. They are prevented from being able to secure a decent return on their work and forced to accept intolerable conditions because otherwise they will not be able to eat.

When people die in order to fatten the purses of the rich, it is murder. If the economic practices of a group of consumers prevent the poor from being able to obtain the means of survival, then the blood of those who are unjustly treated will cry out to the Lord. And the Old Testament repeatedly assures us that He will hear and answer their plea for vengeance.

SELF MADE

God has not created us for the perishable and transitory things of earth, but for things heavenly and everlasting; He has given us this world as a place of exile, and not as our abiding place. As for riches and the other things which men call good and desirable, whether we have them in abundance, or are lacking in them — so far as eternal happiness is concerned — it makes no difference; the only important thing is to use them aright.

Rerum Novarum

God prefers variety to equality. The American dream is based on the idea that people are given equal opportunities and that those who succeed, succeed by their own merits, while those who fail, fail through their own fault. This is not true: God has not apportioned abilities, talents, family, culture, or any other form of grace equally to all people. He has deliberately crafted His creation so that there will be the greatest possible diversity. God is an artist, not a factory production line; He is not interested in producing men of uniform quality according to clear specifications but in making unique human beings, each one never before seen and never to be repeated. In order to accomplish this He must apportion His creatures with a wide range of strengths and weaknesses, advantages and deprivations.

To see how absurd this idea of equal opportunity is, let's look at the one area where the State can be relied on to try to legislate equality: equality under the law. This has been an essential concept in statecraft since the ancient world, and in no human state has it ever been accomplished. In America today, for example, if a poor man is arrested, he is less likely to be able to afford competent legal representation than a rich man. A poorly educated man will not know his rights as well as a well-educated one. An articulate man will probably make a better impression on the jury than one who is dull and poorly spoken. A black man is more likely than a white man to be put to death for a capital offense in most states which maintain the death penalty. If the state cannot even secure equality amongst men in the areas where she holds full jurisdiction, how could she possibly obtain it for them in the world at large?

The good things of this world are apportioned unequally, but it does not therefore follow that life is unfair. It is an error for those who are wealthy and successful to believe that they have become so by their own efforts, but it is equally an error for those who are not wealthy or successful to see themselves as victims of society. Both arrogance and envy are sins, and either suffices to make men miserable.

Nothing which is essential to happiness or blessedness is withheld from any seeker. God has promised that if we ask Him for what is good, He will always give it. "Ask, and it will be given to you; search, and you will find; knock, and the door will be opened to you. For the one who asks always receives; the one who searches always finds; the one who knocks will always have the door opened to him. What father among you would hand his son a stone when he asked for bread? ... If you then, who are evil, know how to give your children what is good, how much more will the heavenly Father give the Holy Spirit to those who ask him!" (Luke 11:9-13). Riches are not necessarily good. They often lead to complacency, pride, addiction to luxuries, or other spiritual illnesses.

We must also recall that God must allow some people to be poor, and to be really poor, in order to goad the consciences of those who have chosen to become wealthy by evil means. Some people who suffer poverty must be truly good: if only bad and slothful people were poor, then the rich would seem justified in their pride and in their neglect of the poor. The economy of salvation relies on the innocent suffering in order to save the guilty. "I think it is very beautiful for the poor to accept their lot, to share it with the passion of Christ. I think the world is being much helped by the suffering of the poor people" (Mother Teresa). This seems like pure nonsense to those who measure blessedness in terms of pleasure and wealth: it is foolishness to the hedonists, and a scandal to the socialists. It is, however, the only form of beatitude that Christ ever peddled.

Finally, we should remember that God will often allow people to go on suffering deprivation if the reason that they are in need is that they are too proud to ask another human being for help. One of the primary channels of divine providence is human compassion. A person who has not been negligent in carrying out his duties should not feel ashamed of asking for help. Nor should those who are asked feel imposed upon. To be given riches is a privilege, not because it allows a person to enjoy all sorts of sensual luxuries, but because it allows him the joy of being helpful to others.

MAKE SELF

*Men always work harder and more readily when they work on
that which belongs to them; nay, they learn to love the very soil
that yields in response to the labor of their hands, not only food
to eat, but an abundance of good things for themselves and those
that are dear to them.*

Rerum Novarum

I would like to contrast two board games, both of
which are models of economic life. The first is the most
popular and widely available board game in the world;
everyone has played it, and it is called Monopoly. The second
is one of the best board games in the world, as judged by
board game enthusiasts, and it is called Agricola.

Monopoly is a game in which you are a rapacious
landowner. The goal is to amass as much wealth as possible
until all of the other players are broke and you own
everything. Agricola is a game in which you are a recently
married couple working a small farm. The goal is to have the
most successful farm as measured by a diverse set of
objectives that measure how effectively you have used your
land.

At the beginning of Monopoly, everyone is thrust into
a square, uniform world in which they are compelled to go
around and around endlessly until they either gain or lose
everything. Values in this world are fixed and arbitrary: there
is nothing that makes Boardwalk more valuable than
Connecticut Avenue, it just is. Players in Agricola are given a
little piece of land with a small house on it, a private world
which they are expected to cultivate. Players choose to assign

different values and purposes to the different parts of their property to impress their personalities and choices onto it.

In Monopoly, there is only one strategy for winning the game: manipulate the other players into making trades which are advantageous to oneself, and disadvantageous to the other. All things being equal, the most cunning player will always win, though there is a strong element of chance that can sometimes upset the balance in favor of the second most cunning player. The strategy in Agricola is sufficiently complex and varied from game to game that it cannot be summarized so succinctly. However, in so far as there is a general principle that offers an advantage every time, it is to be the first to have children. In Monopoly children make 4 cameo appearances in connection with such things as school tax and hospital tax.

The currency in Monopoly is cash which is infused into the games economy by the mysterious "GO" square whenever a player completes a lap of the rat race without being accosted by law enforcement. The unit of currency in Agricola is time, which is then converted into food, housing, resources, and upgrades.

Money is used in Monopoly to buy up other people's homes and the necessities of life, which are then "improved" by building uniform houses and hotels on them. The only purpose of these improvements is to make more money. In Agricola, resources are spent to create new means of production and increase self-sufficiency.

These games model two different systems of economic life: monopolistic capitalism and universal private land ownership. It is not by accident that the Vatican consistently favors the latter: it produces a world in which people are granted the greatest possible scope for creativity and personality, while encouraging the production of reasonable quantities of high-quality goods.

One of the advantages of becoming detached from the consumerist cycle is that it leaves time and money free for a person to establish a higher degree of self-directed work. Instead of spending money on impulse buys or luxuries, one can think rationally about how best to invest in one's own productive capacities by purchasing the tools and equipment necessary to enter into small-scale production. A person who invests in his own skills and who makes things for himself will be able to enjoy unique goods at a massively reduced price, and will also be enabled to create truly meaningful gifts to share with the community at large.

Goods that you make yourself are far better than goods that you buy because they have all of their value intact. There is not only the value associated with the use of the good, but also the pleasure of having produced it, the gratitude to the earth for the resources that it has supplied, and the joy of improving one's abilities. Self-made products are also always perfectly conformed to the aesthetic preferences and practical needs of the person who makes them or to those of the person to whom they are gifted. These goods establish a relationship with the land and with other people that more closely resembles the relationships of mutual giving that existed in the Beginning.

LOW INTEREST

Set your hearts on his kingdom first, and on his righteousness, and all these other things will be given you as well.

Matthew 6:33

Time is not a uniform creature. The invention of the clock and of an entire edifice of scientific and technological progress that relies on the uniformity of time have led people to think of it as a basically linear substance through which one is dragged at a constant pace. This conception of temporality replaced a religious understanding of time as a creative medium capable of being impregnated with significance and value. The difference between these two notions of time is the difference between 12:00pm and lunchtime or 12:00am and the witching hour.

The modern world has a tremendous number of institutions and edifices designed to govern human time according to a predictable chronological order. Just as modernism attempted to govern space according to very exacting and predictable models, it now attempts to govern time in the same way. Children are taught this schematic view of temporality from a very young age: our educational institutions break down tasks not according to what must be accomplished, but according to the numbers on the clock. This way of interacting with time feels natural to modern man only because it is inculcated into him at such an early stage in his development. In fact it is quite counterintuitive: it is much more natural to break up time according to tasks that must be accomplished and to move from one task to the next upon completion rather than at some arbitrarily appointed moment in the diurnal cycle.

Factory labor cannot proceed without the punch-clock because it is endless. The tasks are never complete. This kind of labor is the full realization of an entire conception of work which proceeds from the invention of the clock, and the impregnation of that conception into the field of labor. This labor is uniform not only in terms of the hour, but also in terms of the day, and the season. A holiday, or holy day, is an unnatural break in this perpetual flow of standardized productivity. Time is converted into goods, which are converted into money at a perpetual and predictable rate. In this way, the value of a moment becomes measurable in currency.

The influence of this rationalization of time on the human psyche is profound. Let's contrast it for a moment with the medieval system of time-telling. According to that schema, time was bound up in spiritual meanings. The various times of day were told according to "hours," each of which had a particular set of prayers and rituals associated with it. The procession of days was broken up according to a liturgical calendar in which there was a constant fluctuation in the value of time: certain days were merely "the Monday after the 2nd Sunday in ordinary time," while others were "the Solemnity of the Annunciation." This ebb and flow of rich time vs. poor time, time that was pregnant with meaning vs. ordinary time, meant that people were constantly living through a temporal landscape broken up by familiar landmarks. Time was constantly telling itself as a story, a series of linked events which brought each other into focus and which provided a sense of narrative artistry to the very act of living in time.

Associated with this conceptualization of the temporal was an entire field of techniques for doing things at "the right time." "There is a season for everything, a time for every occupation under heaven" (Eccles 3:1). The time for making money, for sending out ships, for planting a field, for reaping a harvest, for building, for making war, or the time for withdrawing into the desert each had its place within the framework of a human life. This meant that work which did not have a financial reward, the work of monks, for example, or of the leisured classes, still had a concrete and discernible value within the context of society. It could be evaluated according to a different set of criteria completely without reference to its material productivity.

Without the existence of a rich set of criteria for evaluating the application of time, money quickly becomes the lowest common denominator that defines whether or not time is being spent in a worthwhile manner. Instead of leisure time, people have "down time" or "time off," just enough that they can rest and get back to work. Even then, leisure pursuits are required to justify themselves in monetary terms: education becomes a means of securing a better job, socialization becomes networking, the arts become a vehicle for advertising. Time at work is measured in the same terms, and people end up valuing their work not in terms of its products or its purposes, but merely in terms of the hourly wage. This causes people to willingly forgo opportunities to do things which they love and which provide them with a sense of deep satisfaction, because they would rather have a better paying position. The fact that things are beautiful, meaningful, and interesting in and of themselves ceases to be a sufficient reason for pursuing them.

It is a mistake to think of this primarily as a consequence of individual avarice. People have a deep, ingrained impulse to work to serve the common good, and they will naturally seek validation for their work through practices of cultural valuation. It is very difficult to feel justified in pursuing ends which society does not explicitly value. In a culture where the value of time and the value of life are measured primarily in economic terms, people feel morally compelled to spend their time in the most efficient possible way in order to produce economic rewards. Time that does not serve the improvement of one's "quality of life" or "standard of living" as measured in monetary terms is seen as a "waste of time," a frivolous and probably slothful luxury. As a result, men and women in all good conscience become enslaved to boredom and tedium, their lives slowly ground up in Mammon's golden jaw.

HIGH FIDELITY

Goods of production — material or immaterial — such as land, factories, practical or artistic skills, oblige their possessors to employ them in ways that will benefit the greatest number. Those who hold goods for use and consumption should use them with moderation, reserving the better part for guests, for the sick and the poor.

CCC 2405

Every person is a unique manifestation of the image and likeness of God. Through work, man "cooperates with [God] in completing the work of creation and engraving on the earth the spiritual imprint which he himself has received" (*Gaudium et Spes*). Creation is God's masterpiece; every human being is both a part of the work and also a co-creator, one who helps to bring it into existence. All of our work is ultimately directed towards the final product: the New Heaven and the New Earth where all things will be reconciled in Christ and made new.

This means that the true import of work does not lie in its material products. The material elements of the present creation are all perishable. This world is the nursery in which souls are being formed, and the material goods of the Earth contribute to that formation in much the same way that toys contribute to the formation of a child. When a child plays, it is not a waste of time but rather a rehearsal in which he acts out the roles that he will play as a man. Likewise, a man plays with earthly goods, acting out the role that he will play as a saint.

It sometimes happens that a child does not have fun with his toys. He becomes angry because a block tower will not hold together or because he is unable to draw a dog with the correct proportions. He screws up his little face, and stomps his feet, and declares the game to be stupid. People are like this throughout life: they end up thinking of earthly toils as something terribly serious and lose their sense of joy and fun, the wonder of being able to use all of the faculties which God has given them. Life, the body, the will, moral responsibilities, and rational intelligence are seen as burdens which must be shouldered grudgingly or else neglected in order to obtain freedom. The sense that everything is a beautiful gift which contributes to making a masterpiece of a human life is lost.

Work is a means of developing the self, not an end in itself. When Paul VI describes the process of production he draws our attention towards the spiritual ends of work. "Bent over a material that resists his efforts, the worker leaves his imprint on it, at the same time developing his own powers of persistence, inventiveness and concentration. Further, when work is done in common — when hope, hardship, ambition and joy are shared — it brings together and firmly unites the wills, minds and hearts of men. In its accomplishment, men find themselves to be brothers" (*Populorum Progressio*). The meaning and purpose of work is the development of persistence, inventiveness, unity, brotherhood and so forth. The products are secondary.

God does not envision His creation as one soviet people, united into a sort of gray, indiscriminate, and interchangeable proletariat, so He gives different work to different people, encouraging the development of a variety of charisms and virtues. "Now you together are Christ's body; but each of you is a different part of it. In the Church, God has given the first place to apostles, the second to prophets, the third to teachers; after them, miracles, and after them the gift of healing; helpers, good leaders, those with many languages. Are all of them apostles, or all of them prophets, or all of them teachers? Do they all have the gift of miracles, or all have the gift of healing? Do all speak strange languages, and all interpret them?" (1 Cor 12:27-30). In order for this body to work, however, it is necessary that each of the parts knows what role it is to play and pursues the purpose for which it was made. If the big toe woke up one morning and decided to migrate up to the face in order to become an eye (believing that eyes were more dignified and prestigious than big toes), it would succeed neither in seeing nor in balancing the foot and would only become an unsightly blemish.

Discerning what to do with one's life is a matter of two interrelated processes. On the one hand, it is important to discern the will of God. On the other, it is important to exercise free will. Some people focus neurotically on doing the will of God and end up living in anxious inactivity watching for signs and portents to reassure them that what they're doing is right. This produces a superstitious outlook and generally leads to unhappiness, mostly because this sort of person tends to assume that the will of God is contrary to their own will and that anything which brings them happiness and joy must secretly be based on disordered self-interest.

The opposite error is to think only of oneself in choosing a vocation. The desire for self-aggrandizement of one sort or another leads many people to neglect their true vocation in order to pursue vainglorious ambitions. Such people are usually neither successful nor happy: someone who becomes an actor because they wish to be famous will generally act unconvincingly, and a person who becomes a philosopher because they wish to appear clever will attain little wisdom.

In trying to discern God's will, it is helpful to remember that Christ and the soul are espoused. Look at St. Paul's description of the relationship between a husband and a wife: "Husbands should love their wives just as Christ loved the Church and sacrificed himself for her to make her holy" (Eph 5:25). The obedience of the soul to God is always undertaken in the recognition that what God wants for a person is exactly identical with that person's good. Talents, aptitudes, skills, desires, hopes, longings, gifts, charisms, weaknesses, needs, limitations, and all of the other conditions that make up a human life are a part of the equation. Freedom is a part of the equation as well: a good husband doesn't just order his wife around, he finds out what she most deeply wants and then helps her to achieve that.

The most useful way to discern God's will is not to sit around and pray about it for a long time. There are people who waste years of their lives praying to know the will of God, waiting for a sign, terrified to move in any direction for fear that it might not be right. God can't work with that. Imagine that a child approaches her father and says, "What should I do with my life? What should I become?" The first question that any good father will ask is "Well, what would you like to do?" If the child shuffles her feet and says anxiously, "I just want to do whatever will make you happy," her father will be at a loss. The child has everything upside down. A good father is not interested in having his child pour out her life as an oblation to his own desires. He wants to see his child enjoy the fruits of self-determination and responsibility.

Doing the will of God is a matter of cultivating the right attitude, and this includes the humility to risk getting it wrong. Someone who is practicing virtue and who has prayed to do God's will, just has to start moving forward. If they're heading towards ruin and disaster, God will give them a nudge in the right direction. A sheep that is on the move is easy to shepherd, but a terrified sheep that is standing in place and won't go in any direction is impossible to guide.

LOOSE CHANGE

You must bring the best of the first-fruits of your soil to the house of Yahweh your God.

Exodus 23:19

All money and wealth come from God. The Mosaic code was very specific about the ways in which the faithful were to return to God His share of what they had been given. The first fruits of the field and the herd were to be brought and sacrificed to God, and ten percent was to be taken off the top of one's earnings and placed at the service of the almighty. A man who owned a farm or a vineyard was not allowed to go over their fields twice: anything that was missed on the first pass was to be left so that the widows and orphans and strangers could go and glean there. Debts were forgiven on a cyclical basis. Donations for the needs of the poor and the priesthood were clearly prescribed in the law.

The new covenant did away with all of these legal prescriptions, but it did not do away with the obligations that motivated them. When Saint Paul describes the collections that he is taking up from various different churches, he makes it clear that the early Christians were in a sort of competition with one another, each trying to outdo the others in generosity (see 2 Cor 8-9). In the book of Acts, the description of the Church is of a community in which people literally give up everything for the sake of the common good. "None of their members was ever in want, as all those who owned land or houses would sell them, and bring the money from them, to present it to the apostles; it was then distributed to any members who might be in need" (Acts 4:34-35). The strict letter of the Law was abolished, not in order that people could give less, but in order that people would willingly and cheerfully give more: "Do not imagine that I have come to abolish the Law or the Prophets. I have come not to abolish but to complete them" (Matt 5:17).

It is a great scandal that today, in the richest countries of the world, churches are forced to pay their bills by hosting Bingo Night; that many beautiful old churches have become tourist traps because it is the only way that they can afford to maintain their premises; that modern churches are chintzy and ugly looking because there is not enough money to buy stained glass windows or to use building materials more attractive than concrete blocks; that magnificent pipe organs sit gathering dust because parishes cannot afford to hire organists. If we were all traipsing to church in bare feet, dressed in the patched-up rags of our Sunday best this might be excusable; but most people arrive in nice cars and spend more on cable TV than they spend to maintain the house of God.

Look at the example that Christ uses when He wishes to teach His disciples about the spirit of generosity. A woman comes up and puts two small coins into the Temple treasury. Christ says, "I tell you solemnly, this poor widow has put more in than all who have contributed to the treasury; for they have all put in money they had over, but she from the little she had has put in everything she possessed, all she had to live on" (Mark 12:43-44). Saint Paul says the same of the Macedonians when he is trying to spur the Corinthians to greater acts of sacrifice for his collection: "throughout great trials, by suffering, their constant cheerfulness and their intense poverty have overflowed in a wealth of generosity. I can swear that they gave not only as much as they could afford, but far more, and quite spontaneously, begging and begging us for the favor of sharing in this service of the saints" (2 Cor 8:2-5). Although "this does not mean that to give relief to others you ought to make things difficult for yourselves" (2 Cor 8:13), there is the strong suggestion that those who do so will be rewarded for their generosity.

Most people, however, are a long way off from donating more than they can reasonably afford. There is a sad presentation each year in most parishes where the head of the finance committee gets on their hind legs and reads out the annual report. In most places, regardless of the social conditions of the parishioners, the offertory envelopes fall short of the most basic needs of the parish. Bingo nights and lotteries are necessary just to pay the bills and prevent the buildings from falling down. Beautifying the House of God through investment in the arts and improving parish outreach to the larger community are simply impossible on such a shoestring budget. This could not possibly be construed as putting aside legalistic concerns in order to better fulfill the spirit of the Law.

People in the modern world tend to throw the Church the dregs of their fortunes. This means that during the Offertory, when we are preparing to receive the Body and Blood of Christ which He poured out for us without measure, we are telling God that He is an afterthought. Contrast this with the state of mind demanded by the Mosaic law: the people would wait all season for the ewes or the cows to bring forth their offspring. The animals would calve in the spring, following on the hard months of winter when people were struggling to survive on the remains of last year's harvest. The first spring lamb would come forth from its mother's womb — and it would be taken and sacrificed to the Lord. The first fruits, not the leftovers, were given to God.

Those who honestly cannot afford to give much money should look for other ways to provide for the Church. This can include giving time to help with building projects, giving artistic or musical talents, helping out with the visitation of the sick and the elderly, baking or contributing goods to church fundraisers, and perhaps most importantly, opening the womb and the home to provide the Church with a new generation of children.

The Church is our mother. Just as Christ placed His mother in the care of St. John the Divine from the Cross, so He places the Church in the care of all the faithful today.

DIMINISHING RETURNS

Sheol and Perdition are never satisfied, nor are the eyes of man ever satisfied.

Proverbs 27:20

In the past, people lived in a more or less fixed social class. Saint Thomas Aquinas said that people should live in a manner that was seemly for their station, which was a reasonable thing to say in a society where stations were clearly defined and where a seemly standard could be easily determined. St. Thomas's advice could be used to work out a clearly-defined, constant standard of living beyond which any desires would obviously be disordered. Not so in a society where social mobility is taken as a norm. In this cultural context, social class is largely determined by the way that a person chooses to live. It is possible to join a different social circle merely by amassing more wealth or spending more money.

The argument from living according to one's station is now sometimes used to justify a certain degree of luxurious living amongst the well-off in the modern world. The argument runs as follows: if you look, live, and entertain like a tramp, you won't be able to effectively evangelize people in the higher classes. Those people also have a right to be evangelized. Therefore, Catholics who are well off should maintain themselves in a manner that will make them acceptable to other people in their social circle. I'm a bit skeptical about this argument. If someone really had an effective ministry to the rich, and it required them to appear well-off, then I think that this argument would stand, but in many cases folks who make this argument are just as afraid of offending others in their social circle by openly talking about their faith as they are afraid of looking poor. In such cases, it's just an excuse to salve the conscience. A second reason that I'm leery of this argument is that the saints who were really rich, people like St. Francis of Assisi and St. Elizabeth of Hungary, evangelized others in their class not by living sumptuously but by putting aside wealth for the sake of the Kingdom of Heaven. Yes, Francis was a mendicant friar, but Elizabeth was a married laywoman. Finally, I think it is difficult to evangelize people who are in the clutches of avarice by also appearing to be in the clutches of avarice. Imagine that a woman said, "I have to dress in revealing clothes, flirt with many men, and go to the club every weekend, because that's how I evangelize people who are addicted to casual sex." It's a weird and wonderful world, and maybe there is someone who could actually make this work, but to me it seems a bit dubious.

Witnessing to a culture obsessed with consumption would seem to require the mortification of the desire to consume. The blind cannot lead the blind, and if Christians do not detach themselves from the mechanisms of desire and acquisition, then we will not be able to bring down the Culture of Death or build up a Culture of Life. I think it is a mistake to think of the Culture of Death primarily in terms of abortion and contraception: these practices were originally made acceptable to North Americans by appeals to money. Poor families needed condoms because they could not afford more children; women needed abortions because having babies forced them into poverty. Even today, the promulgation of anti-population strategies in the third world is justified almost entirely in terms of economics: only the most die-hard feminists think that African women need birth control so that they can attain sexual liberation. Most people think that Africans need birth control because the world can't afford to feed any more black babies.

So how do we go about disentangling ourselves? The first step towards overcoming any sinful habit is to avoid occasions of sin. In the case of consumerism this is very difficult: occasions of sin, in the form of advertising, confront us every time that we walk down the street or turn on a computer.

Advertising is specifically designed to have an effect on people even if they are consciously dedicated to ignoring its messages. Most people just absorb it unthinkingly, but even if you know that you are being manipulated, it still hits the subconscious and provides fodder for covetous inclinations. Western society exposes a person to literally millions of advertisements every day. There are people whose lives are devoted to making these advertisements influence human behavior, and they have become very, very good at it. A lot of advertising cannot be avoided, but one of the most common sources is broadcast TV — which can. Watching television not only tends to waste leisure time, it also programs the viewer to buy mass-market junk.

This doesn't mean that all television is bad, but when it is good, the advertising is a form of vandalism. Good TV shows are works of art: the ads break tension, diminish emotional impact, and prevent the viewer from being able to fully appreciate the work. Fortunately, most shows can be downloaded online or obtained on DVD, making it possible to skip the commercials.

Avoiding advertising is not easy, but it is vitally important because almost all advertising involves either explicit or implicit deception. Coke does not give life, nor is there any brand of yoghurt that will make a man fatally attractive to supermodels. Being lied to is unpleasant; it is an act of violence against truth, and it wounds the intellect. When the mind is constantly inundated with lies, it will either come to believe them, or it will become hostile and cynical towards all truth claims. Both the avid consumerism of

90

popular culture and the jaded ironicism of intellectual culture are the products of the ubiquity of advertising. The effects are not only seen in the commercial sphere, but also in the spiritual realm: if words and concepts like "love," "freedom," "joy," "happiness," and "beauty" are constantly used to flog substandard commercial schlock, the words themselves lose their ability to communicate their true meanings. Most of us are so accustomed to being buffeted by these constant lies that we no longer perceive it as painful, but that does not mean that we can't regain our interior health and equilibrium by distancing ourselves from the sources of consumerist blather.

GOLD STANDARD

Your wealth is all rotting, your clothes are all eaten up by moths. All your gold and your silver are corroding away, and the same corrosion will be your own sentence, and eat into your body. It was a burning fire that you stored up as your treasure for the last days.

James 5:2-6

The universal wisdom of the world is that one of the things which every man ought to do in order to secure his life against financial loss is to hoard up money for himself. Once upon a time this was done rather romantically: people would put their gold into chests, and they would bury the chests in secret places in the ground. Eventually, if they felt sufficiently poor, they would go out and dig the chests up. "A strange madness, that," said St. Basil the Great, "when gold lies hidden with other metals, one ransacks the earth; but after it has seen the light of day, it disappears again beneath the ground. From this, I perceive, it happens to you that in burying your money you bury also your heart. 'For where your treasure is,' it is said, 'there will your heart be also' (Matt 6:21)."

People today generally don't bury gold. Money is no longer made of precious metals, but of numbers in computers, so people bury their wealth in banks where they hope that it will remain, waiting to be dug up in a time of need. Christ warns against this practice: "There was once a rich man who, having had a good harvest from his land, thought to himself, 'What am I to do? I have not enough room to store my crops.' Then he said, 'This is what I will do. I will pull down my barns and build bigger ones, and store all my grain and my goods in them, and I will say to my soul: My soul, you have plenty of good things laid by for many years to come; take things easy, eat, drink, have a good time.' But God said to him, 'Fool! This very night the demand will be made for your soul; and this hoard of yours, whose will it be then?' So it is when a man stores up treasure for himself in place of making himself rich in the sight of God" (Luke 12:16-21).

Surely this can't be right. The man in this parable has acted very sensibly and prudently: he has put away a little nest egg and made preparation for the future. Surely Christ is only saying that this is problematic because the man is self-satisfied. He's not saying that we shouldn't provide for the future in case of difficulties that may arise.

On the contrary, the excess goods that I have now are things which someone else needs. If I keep those things because I might need them later, then I am keeping them back from their proper owners.

Christian social teaching is difficult because it involves trusting in an invisible hand, not the invisible hand of the marketplace, but the invisible hand of providence. "Give, and there will be gifts for you: a full measure, pressed down, shaken together, and running over, will be poured into your lap" (Luke 6:38). If I keep my riches close to me, buried in the ground, invested in the bank, or cleverly concealed behind the wallpaper in my living room, then I know where they are when I need them. If I send my wealth out into the world, for all I know it will never come back. There is nothing certain, nothing guaranteed, just some abstract theological principle.

The abstract theological principle is a promise made by God. The problem that people have with Christ's hard sayings about money is that Christ seems to be under the impression that God is more trustworthy than the bank. It's one thing to go to church and talk about believing in Jesus, to take Pascal's wager and put down a few chips on God to make sure that if the big gamble pays off you'll be collecting dividends in Heaven. It's another thing to bet everything you have on the Big Invisible Man in the Sky. You could get burned. You could give and give and give out of the store of your riches and end up poor and unprovided for if it turns out that God doesn't exist.

Unfortunately, God is not interested in the faith of those who hedge their bets. This is why Christ is so worried about the salvation of the rich: "I tell you solemnly, it will be hard for a rich man to enter the kingdom of heaven. Yes, I tell you again, it is easier for a camel to pass through the eye of a needle than for a rich man to enter the kingdom of heaven" (Matt 19:23-24). This saying astonished the disciples, who were poor. It ought to astonish us. Most of us are rich. We'd better wonder why it is that it's going to be easier for a camel to go through the eye of a needle than it will be for us to get into heaven. Fortunately, Christ gives the answer: "For men...this is impossible; for God everything is possible" (Matt 19:26). For a rich person to get into heaven he must have real, concrete faith: he must really believe that God is able to do the impossible.

Giving to those who have been generous is not impossible. It's not even difficult. People who regularly send gifts and goods out into the world, who make it their primary business to provide for the needs of the poor instead of worrying about their own future needs, do not go unrewarded. They draw to themselves communities: family, friends, church, neighbors. People will come forward to help those who have helped them. They will even come forward to help those who have not helped them personally, but who are known to have helped others. If people, who are evil, are able to do this, then how much more will God provide for those who have cared for His little ones?

FIAT CURRENCY

And there is no limit to the blessings which God can send you —
He will make sure that you will always have all you need for
yourselves in every possible circumstance, and still have
something to spare for all sorts of good works.

2 Corinthians 9:8

I don't know what to do about money. As far as I can tell, it's a totally malleable substance of no fixed value, and it's remarkably responsive to spiritual realities. I try to budget, I try to be responsible, I don't spend much. Sometimes, there is plenty of money, no extraordinary expenses, everything is sensibly budgeted for, and it remains almost impossible to make ends meet. Then a couple of months later, income will be low, there will be several unexpected expenses, the budgeting will look ghastly, and somehow, the money just won't run out. The only pattern that I have been able to discover is that money is tight when I'm worried about money, and it's free-flowing when I'm indifferent to it.

I'm not sure that money works this way for everyone. I'm assuming that some people have been given gifts of financial acuity and commercial prowess, and perhaps for those people money behaves more like it does in economics text books. I am not one of those people, and so far as I can tell, God does not intend for me to become one. Whenever I try to do it all myself, it's a flop. Whenever I put it in His hands, it all works, and I don't know how.

There is one story in the gospel that seems to partially explain this. Some men come from the Temple collecting the annual Temple tax. Neither Jesus nor St. Peter has any money, and St. Peter's not sure what they're going to do about it. Christ says: "Go to the lake and cast a hook; take the first fish that bites, open its mouth and there you will find a shekel; take it and give it to them for me and for you" (Matt 17:27). Neither Christ nor St. Peter have made any advance preparation or budgeted for the Temple tax, and they haven't kept a bit of money in the bank in case they need it for a rainy day. They suddenly find themselves in need, so Christ sends Peter out to do his ordinary, day-to-day work. Peter works, and the money appears more or less miraculously, and that's the end of the story.

God expects people to do the things that they are good at. He always provides the means to do those things, so long as He is asked. If I do my work diligently and faithfully, the money is there. If I spend my time worrying about the money and end up ignoring my actual duties and responsibilities in a flurry of fruitless anxiety, then the money will always be short.

I think that a lot of people who have no talent with money end up being poor and anxious for their entire lives because they feel that God expects them to practice a kind of financial acumen that they are not capable of achieving. It is like the story of the three servants: one is given five talents, another two, and the last one only one talent. The one who has not been blessed with much to begin with feels jilted: why were the other servants given so much more? Why was he only given one talent to invest? So, because he resents his position of poverty, he concludes that the master is unjust. He goes and buries his talent in the ground: after all, it's only one stupid talent. How much of a return could he really be expected to get on that? When the master comes back, he's not impressed; he has the one talent seized from the lazy servant, and the servant is cast into the outer darkness to weep and gnash his teeth (see Matt 25:14-30).

If the servant who was only given one talent had just gone out and been faithful with his one talent, then the master would have said, "Well done, good and faithful servant; you have shown you can be faithful in small things, I will trust you with greater; come and join in your master's happiness" (Matt 25:21, 23). What does the servant do instead? He accuses the master: "I had heard you were a hard man, reaping where you have not sown and gathering where you have not scattered" (Matt 25:24). What is he saying? He's saying that if only the master had given him more talents in the first place, he would have been able to get a return, but that the master didn't give him enough for him to really be able to achieve anything — so he didn't bother to try.

God expects people to make use of what He has actually given them, not to spend their lives ignoring their real talents and aptitudes out of mistaken feeling that they would be better able to succeed if only they had someone else's abilities. From those to whom God has not given riches, He does not expect to receive a return on His investment of riches. From those to whom He has not given a talent for making and managing money, He does not expect a return on the making and managing of money. Yet woe to the person who has been given artistic talent, or a genius for mothering, or a green thumb, or a scientific intellect, and who has buried it in the ground because they resent not having been blessed with money.

JUST WAGES

In work, the person exercises and fulfills in part the potential inscribed in his nature. The primordial value of labor stems from man himself, its author and its beneficiary. Work is for man, not man for work.

CCC 2428

It's easy for someone like me, who has the advantage of being able to do meaningful, self-directed work, to look at footage of people in factories and feel outraged. Surely it is not in accord with human dignity to have to do the same thing over and over again all day so that someone else can profit from it. It seems so menial, so dreary, so unjust. How can this sort of labor, in which a person is turned into a cog in a machine, possibly be reconciled with the Church's teachings on the dignity of work?

Paul VI makes an interesting observation: "If it is true that a type of capitalism, as it is commonly called, has given rise to hardships, unjust practices, and fratricidal conflicts that persist to this day, it would be a mistake to attribute these evils to the rise of industrialization itself, for they really derive from the pernicious economic concepts that grew up along with it. We must in all fairness acknowledge the vital role played by labor systematization and industrial organization in the task of development" (*Populorum Progressio*). We have here the outline of a solution to my conundrum. It is not the industrial process that is evil, but these "pernicious economic concepts." So what are these concepts?

The Vatican points towards several possible culprits. The problems of rampant individualism and of socialism are well documented, but there is also a third problem: Benedict XVI in *Caritas in Veritate* speaks of "technocracy," literally rule by technology. One of the economic concepts that arose at the same time as the industrial revolution was the idea of a technologically organized society. According to certain Enlightenment ideals, people could become infinitely more productive and efficient if they could be turned into living machines. Reading about them now is somewhat surreal: it's difficult to believe that people actually believed this stuff. Writers in the 18th and 19th centuries could really whip themselves up into a fury of excitement about the possibility of a social order that had been entirely systematized and regularized. The Prussians, who led the charge, envisioned an army that functioned literally like a group of tin soldiers that could be wound up and marched into battle in absolute and perfect uniformity. They sought to organize society according to rigidly defined scientific principles, in order to regulate and therefore control all human activity. The situation was so extreme that for a time Prussian women were obliged to report their menstrual cycles to the government.

The philosopher Jeremy Bentham developed an architectural concept which he felt would allow for this kind of regularized society. He called it the "panopticon," a building in which individuals would be compartmentalized into small cells arranged around a central tower in which an invisible authority would be able to observe all of their activities. Originally intended as a design for prisons, Bentham and his followers quickly proceeded to enthuse about the advantages which it could provide in schools, hospitals, and factories. Some dreamed of entire cities arranged according to a panoptic scheme, albeit with a more sophisticated web of surveillance. In this environment, crime would be impossible. Sloth would be eliminated. Human nature would finally submit itself perfectly to the dictates of reason — not individual reason, mind, but Reason as defined by the technocrats who would rule this clockwork paradise.

The fruits of this worldview are still in evidence today, and they are responsible for many evils. Although the planned economies of the Soviet Union proved to be a complete failure, the notion of top-down social regimentation continues to be a feature of many national and international policies. This violates the principle of subsidiarity, which is an essential feature of Catholic social teaching. Subsidiarity is the idea that power should be diffused as widely as possible and that higher forms of organization should serve to safeguard the powers and authorities of lower forms of organization. This kind of organization gives the broadest possible scope for individual moral responsibility and prevents the systematization of evils.

Individual Catholics can resist technocracy by supporting economic activity that encourages individual autonomy. Small businesses are often driven out of the market because people are drawn in by the convenience of big box stores, but this convenience is illusory. Technocratic retail operations not only treat their employees as cogs in a machine, they treat their customers in the same way. Stores are organized and arranged in a scientifically managed fashion in order to cause shoppers to involuntarily purchase goods which they do not actually want. Detailed studies of irrational human behavior and of the subconscious cues that drive impulse purchases have been used to deliberately create conditions in which a person is not able to engage rationally with their environment. The result is the creation of commercial spaces which are theoretically convenient, because you can get everything in one place, but which are practically inconvenient, because shoppers consistently end up coming out of the door with a cartload of goods that they do not want or need and with half of their legitimate shopping list forgotten.

Buying from small-scale retailers may take slightly more time, but it serves to create a community in which a larger number of people are enabled to participate in private ownership. It also saves money because small businessmen rely on customer loyalty to stay in business, so they don't dare assault their customers with the sort of dehumanizing psychological ploys that are used by the conglomerates.

STOCK OPTIONS

The following duties bind the wealthy owner and the employer: not to look upon their work people as their bondsmen, but to respect in every man his dignity as a person ennobled by Christian character.... But to misuse men as though they were things in the pursuit of gain, or to value them solely for their physical powers — that is truly shameful and inhuman.

Rerum Novarum

The Vatican's vision of a revitalized industrialism probably sounds to most workers like a beautiful daydream. Catholics who have the advantage of owning or managing a workplace might be able to enact some of these principles, but what is the poor, lowly laborer supposed to do?

Rerum Novarum did not present a particularly rosy picture of the situation: "Some opportune remedy must be found quickly for the misery and wretchedness pressing so unjustly on the majority of the working class: for the ancient workingmen's guilds were abolished in the last century, and no other protective organization took their place. Public institutions and the laws set aside the ancient religion. Hence, by degrees it has come to pass that working men have been surrendered, isolated and helpless, to the hardheartedness of employers and the greed of unchecked competition." Seventy-three years later, *Gaudium et Spes* was not much cheerier: "While the few enjoy very great freedom of choice, the many are deprived of almost all possibility of acting on their own initiative and responsibility, and often subsist in living and working conditions unworthy of human beings."

102

There are three possible approaches for the working man. The first is to take consolation in the fact that "Christ's labors and sufferings, accepted of His own free will, have marvelously sweetened all suffering and all labor" (*Rerum Novarum*). Those who, for whatever reason, are not in a position where it is possible to escape from the injustice of their circumstances are called to join their sufferings to His. It is these poor, much more than the rich, who are truly the authors of mercy in the social sphere: "A truly merciful person is not one that deliberately gives away superfluous things, but one that forgives those who deprive him of what he needs" (Ilias the Presbyter). This does not have to involve a life of total wretchedness and misery; as the philosophers of antiquity were fond of observing, whatever may happen to a man's body and whatever conditions may beset him, he remains in possession of his reason and his will. Suffering is not necessarily bad. A person who cannot change his external circumstances may find creative and innovative ways of using them to achieve interior goals. Even in the most menial tasks, it is almost always possible to apply intelligence in order to do work more efficiently, and if this cannot be done, it is possible to find ways of doing the work so that it produces growth in virtue or so that it is done simultaneously with some more meaningful creative endeavor.

The second approach is to work towards the reformation of one's own workplace. Labor unions have the power to negotiate on behalf of workers. In some cases, this translates only into wage negotiations: the workers are only concerned with how much they are being paid, and as a result, the company is only concerned with how little it can get away with paying them. There are, however, cases where unions have effectively negotiated for workers to gain part ownership, or even a controlling ownership, in the companies that they work for; where the conditions of work have been a major factor in labor negotiations; and where the unions themselves act to join workers together into a genuine community. It is often easier for an individual to become actively and effectively involved in his labor union than it is to directly lobby company ownership, especially in a larger corporation. Unfortunately, in some cases, the unions themselves have ceased to meaningfully represent the employees that they serve and have taken on interests of their own. In such cases, workers would probably be wise to attempt the reform of their unions.

If the union is not effective or if a person's place of work is not unionized, this is not cause for despair. Situations may arise where it is possible for an individual laborer to offer creative input in the workplace. They may be rare, and they may be limited, but someone who watches out for these opportunities may be able to slowly change the way that management thinks about labor in their place of work. Managers are people too. Some are on petty power trips, but others would genuinely like to be managing human beings instead of zombies. A lot of the time the culture of a workplace is governed by a mutual relationship of antagonism between the workers and the owners, or the laborers and management. Owners and managers expect workers to behave insolently, resentfully, and slothfully, so they implement draconian policies to counteract this. The workers in turn feed into the problem by behaving insolently, resentfully, and slothfully. It is sometimes possible to undermine oppression from the bottom up by bearing it cheerfully and by steadfastly behaving like a human being in the face of an inhuman system. Even if this doesn't ultimately cause an appreciable change in workplace conditions, it is certainly worth the effort, for it will always pay solid dividends of self-respect and growth in virtue.

Finally, the laborer who labors under unjust conditions may refuse his labor. I'm not talking only about collective action, but also about finding other means of employment. Many people are enslaved not by their situation but by their

104

inability or unwillingness to change it. People may do work that they hate because it pays better than the work that they would like to be doing or because they would rather have job security than risk pursuing something that they love. Although quitting a dead-end job without a coherent plan for how to support oneself is generally a bad idea, advance planning and persistent effort can allow people to escape from poorly-paid, unskilled work into more fulfilling avenues of achievement.

STONE BREAD

Some men through acts of charity acquire spiritual wealth by means of material wealth; others renounce their material wealth altogether on becoming aware of the spiritual wealth that is inexhaustible.

Ilias the Presbyter

A story is told of Stalin that he once had a chicken brought to him, savagely tore the feathers out of the bird, and then, when it was standing there, naked and bleeding, fed the animal some grain from his hand. He said that if you hurt an animal, then feed it, it will be loyal to you forever — and that people are the same.

It seems likely that the great Soviet tyrant had read Dostoevsky's brilliant analysis of the three temptations which Christ faced in the desert: "Thou wouldst go into the world, and art going with empty hands, with some promise of freedom which men in their simplicity and their natural unruliness cannot even understand, which they fear and dread — for nothing has ever been more insupportable for a man and a human society than freedom. But seest Thou these stones in this parched and barren wilderness? Turn them into bread, and mankind will run after Thee like a flock of sheep, grateful and obedient, though forever trembling, lest Thou withdraw Thy hand and deny them Thy bread" (Fyodor Dostoevsky, *The Brothers Karamazov*).

Christ, in His earthly ministry, spoke numerous times about bread, water, and the necessities of life. His approach was always the same: "Anyone who drinks the water that I shall give will never be thirsty again: the water that I shall give will turn into a spring inside him, welling up to eternal life" (John 4:13-14). "I am the living bread which has come down from heaven. Anyone who eats this bread will live for ever; and the bread that I shall give is my flesh, for the life of the world" (John 6:51). He uses the earthly concerns of the people to whom He is speaking to draw their gaze upwards, towards their heavenly needs. In the desert, the devil tempts Him to reverse this process, to use spiritual authority to meet physical needs. Christ refuses the offer.

The Church is frequently accused of indifference to the poor because She refuses to behave as if man should live by bread alone. There are atheists who argue with great passion that Blessed Teresa of Calcutta was not in fact a good woman at all, that she took money which could have been used to set up truly effective social programs for the long term alleviation of hunger and used it to buy more nuns. They can't understand why she would have spent her time praying and talking with people who were dying of disease or hunger when she could have been busy figuring out how to feed and heal them. In short, she was engaged in the useless business of saving souls when she ought to have been saving bodies.

Providing for the physical needs of the poor is obviously one of the primary social obligations of a Christian, but when the gospel is interpreted solely as a social document, it loses its soul. Judas, who sold his savior for thirty pieces of silver, was the first to complain that Christ had His priorities on this matter backwards: "Mary brought in a pound of very costly ointment, pure nard, and with it anointed the feet of Jesus, wiping them with her hair; the house was full of the scent of the ointment. Then Judas Iscariot — one of his disciples, the man who was to betray him — said, 'Why wasn't this ointment sold for three hundred denarii, and the money given to the poor?' He said this, not because he cared about the poor, but because he was a thief; he was in charge of the common fund and used to help himself to the contributions. So Jesus said, 'Leave her alone; she had to keep this scent for the day of my burial. You have the poor with you always, you will not always have me'" (John 12:3-8).

People who are troubled in their own conscience will often attempt to assuage their feelings of guilt by accusing others of their own sins. Those who are in the grip of avarice and who use their own wealth primarily for self-serving ends will always turn with ire on someone like Mother Teresa. They have exchanged their own integrity for material gain and are enraged by those who have exchanged material wealth for spiritual integrity.

Those who see human good only in material terms have missed the purpose of human life. Spiritual goods are of greater and more enduring value than mere things: "What wrong does Providence, if he gives the better things to the better men? Is it not better to be modest than to be rich?... Why are you vexed then, man, when you possess the better thing?" (Epictetus). This is not only true for those who are deliberately pursuing virtue; it is objectively true. Material charity is good, but when it neglects the spiritual needs of people and attends only to their bodies, it reduces the dignity of the human person and becomes paternalistic.

Poor people often resent the charity of those who serve them because it is directed against a social problem not towards a human being. Almsgiving truly is good, but it is even better to sit down and speak with the beggar to whom you give. It is true that the homeless are often addicted to drugs or alcohol and that they contribute little to society: this is primarily because they feel rejected and lonely. A Christian who judges them, even if he drops a coin into the hat, solidifies that sense of loneliness. A willingness to sit down on the pavement next to another human being, to see the world from their angle, and to listen costs nothing and means everything.

Almost any suffering can be borne if it is shared; almost any suffering is too much if it is accompanied by loneliness. This is why Mother Teresa and her nuns "wasted" valuable time sitting and praying with the dying. This is why she recruited people who would reach out to other people with their own hands instead of spending donations on lobbying or political activism. She recognized that "man does not live on bread alone but that man lives on everything that comes from the mouth of Yahweh" (Deut 8:3), and she recognized also that as Christians we are called to be the mouth of God in the world.

DAILY GRIND

So do not worry about tomorrow: tomorrow will take care of itself. Each day has enough trouble of its own.

Matthew 6:34

In the Lord's Prayer we are taught to pray, "Give us this day our daily bread." Twice, in short succession, Christ situates the material needs of man in the present, as though to hammer in deeply the point that we are to trust in God for today and let the future take care of itself.

Christ is not condemning all forethought. There are few things that can be accomplished in a single day, so obviously it's prudent to plan ahead. What Christ is warning against is worry: a fruitless concern with the future that distracts people from their legitimate duties in the present. This may take the form of unmanly fear, or it may take the form of disordered hope, depending on individual temperament.

Those who are subject to fear begin by thinking that they are making reasonable preparations against future problems. They envision a problem that could arise and try to take action to prevent it. This is disordered when a) the effort taken to prevent problems is greater than the effort that would be required to solve them if they arose, b) the effort spent preventing unlikely eventualities leads to neglect of present duties, or c) worry leads to meddling in matters which are other peoples' responsibility.

A person who is plagued by fears and anxieties about the future should find someone with a more easy-going temperament and submit to their judgment in determining whether their fears are reasonable or not. Irrational fears generally will not flee the moment that their irrationality is revealed, and trying to violently shut them out of one's thoughts is usually ineffectual. Instead, the anticipated suffering should be accepted: pray, as Christ did in Gethsemane, "Father...if you are willing, take this cup away from me. Nevertheless, let your will be done, not mine" (Luke 22:42-43). Ninety-nine times out of a hundred, the fearful premonition will not come to pass; however when fears are used in this way they become opportunities to better resign oneself to the real sufferings that providence will send.

Disordered hope usually takes the form of daydreams. A person envisions future successes and becomes attached to them in advance. Over time, the fantasy takes the place of effort: instead of working towards goals, one fixates on pleasant anticipation of harvests that have not been sown. This creates a relationship of anxiety with the present. There is no limit to what a person can imagine himself accomplishing, and so daydreams will tend to become increasingly elaborate and unrealistic over time. Soon, any real effort seems futile — no matter how hard one works, it is never possible to approach the sort of unimpeded pleasures and successes that haunt the fantasy world.

Idle daydreams can best be conquered by deliberately grounding them. Instead of imagining unlikely future scenarios, a person should imagine breaking down his goals into manageable pieces and then proceed to imagine how he would go about taking the first step towards them. "Nothing is very hard to do" (John Taylor Gatto), but nothing at all can be accomplished in the future. Human beings are able to act only in the present, and so that is where they must live and that is where they must direct their efforts. The only way that a person can interact with the future at all is by making choices in the present that will prepare him for the days to come.

Prudent preparation involves realistically assessing problems that may arise and readying the soul for them in

111

advance. The prudent man who wishes to secure himself against future hardship mentally and morally exercises himself so that when the contest comes he is ready. "It is circumstances which show what men are. Therefore when a difficulty falls upon you, remember that God, like a trainer of wrestlers, has matched you with a rough young man. 'For what purpose?' you may say. Why, that you may become an Olympic conqueror; but it is not accomplished without sweat" (Epictetus).

A soul strengthened in faith, a heart trained in love, a reason exercised in truth, and a will practiced in virtue will suffice to bring a man happiness in the midst of any financial hardship. The joys of Heaven, which lie in the future, will manifest themselves in the present, transforming the world into the image and likeness of paradise. Hardships will dissolve into inconveniences, sufferings become obstacle courses, and poverty will become a transparent pane through which the face of God can be seen.

FAIR PLAY

When he laid down the foundations of the earth, I was by his side, a master craftsman, delighting him day after day, ever at play in his presence, at play everywhere in the world, delighting to be with the sons of men.

Proverbs 8:29-31

You cannot serve both God and Mammon. There are numerous publications on the market that attempt to reconcile Christianity with avarice by showing how to harness biblical wisdom in order to achieve financial wealth. It has always struck me as somehow fitting that these manuals of scripturally justified worldly wisdom tend to rely heavily on writings and proverbs attributed to Solomon the Wise. Yet if we look at the book of Ecclesiastes, which is traditionally understood to be the apotheosis of Solomon's thought, what does the great king say about money? "I amassed silver and gold, the treasures of kings and provinces; acquired singing men and singing women and every human luxury, chest on chest of it. So I grew great, greater than anyone in Jerusalem before me; nor did my wisdom leave me. I denied my eyes nothing they desired, refused my heart no pleasure, a heart that found all my hard work a pleasure; such was the return I got for all my efforts. I then reflected on all that my hands had achieved and on all the effort I had put into its achieving. What vanity it all is, and chasing of the wind!" (2:8-11). Solomon, having accomplished everything, concludes that all of the wealth, luxury, and fame that a man might gain for himself amount to nothing. It is all vanity, all empty, all futile.

This is why Christ tells us not to serve Mammon. It's not because He wishes to deprive us of the means of happiness and pleasure but because He understands that it is impossible for a man to serve two masters. Generally one master has more than enough work to keep his slaves busy throughout the day. A slave who is trying to do the will of two masters at once will either find himself overextended, worn down and exhausted by a double portion of work, or he will constantly have to choose which master to serve and which to neglect. Christ knew that Mammon is a hard master who exploits his slaves for everything that they are worth, feeds them on crumbs, goads them with false promises, and drives them with the whip until they are in the grave. God, on the other hand, is a Master who not only frees His slaves but also offers them adoption as heirs of His household. He is not actually offering a choice between two different kinds of slavery, but rather offering freedom to those who are in chains.

All of this would have had a much more immediate meaning for Christ's interlocutors in the first century, because slavery was a clear and present danger throughout the Empire. Slavery was not, however, the same thing in Rome as it was in the American South. It was not based on a racist notion of innate inferiority, but rather on an elitist understanding of human dignity. Slavery was thus a fate that could befall anyone who was not a Roman citizen, and it was also a state from which men were routinely freed. The Stoic Epictetus, for example, actually was a slave for many years before finally obtaining his freedom and becoming a teacher and philosopher. The risk of slavery, and the reality of freedom, were both possibilities which were a part of the everyday consciousness of men living at the time of Christ.

This experience of literally being put into chains and of literally being released from them formed an important backdrop to a lot of Greco-Roman thought. The great thinkers of the classical world came to the conclusion that happiness could not depend on external circumstances, political slavery or political freedom, but rather on an interior state of self-

114

possession which could not be eradicated by external influences. To understand this in a contemporary context we might think of someone like Solzhenitsyn who lived through the horrors of the Russian gulag system under Stalin. Those who have genuinely experienced a loss of external freedom present an eloquent witness to the importance of the interior freedom which ensures the dignity of the human person regardless of his condition.

The notion of happiness that arises within this context is not an ideal of comfort and wealth but an ideal of *eudaimonia*, greatness of spirit. We are not put here in order to provide ourselves with palliative care in the form of financial success and worldly pleasures until we are finally put out of our misery by death. The world is a vale of soul-making, a place in which heroes are forged. The great insight of Christianity is that this calling is not reserved for the elite. It's not only the thrice-born, the Brahmans, or the male citizens of Athens who are called to accomplish great things. Every person, regardless of their station, is called to be a hero in the divine drama. Greatness is not for the highborn but for the homeless babe born in a manger and wrapped in swaddling clothes.

The call to serve God instead of Mammon is a call to embrace freedom in order to become saints. This doesn't mean that we have to become drippy, pious, church mice slavishly imitating the one-dimensional models of sanctity that tend to be promulgated in Catholic bookstores and sentimental religious art. The difference between a slave and a son is that slaves are interchangeable whereas children are unique. Mammon is not interested in individuality. He wants laboring slaves who are able to operate uniform machines to a uniform standard according to a uniform punch clock, and he wants slavish consumers whose personalities can be reduced to market niches. God wants diversity. He is truly interested in each of His children, for each of us is a unique reflection of

115

Divine Wisdom. Just as a father delights to see his children play and delights in the spontaneity and originality of their joy, so God delights in the people that He has made.

WELL FARE

He humbled you, he made you feel hunger, he fed you with manna which neither you nor your fathers had known, to make you understand that man does not live on bread alone but that man lives on everything that comes from the mouth of Yahweh.

Deuteronomy 8:3

Poverty really is blessed. One of the difficulties that people face in trying to practice virtue is that we tend to think of it in negative terms: thou shalt not do this; thou shalt not do that. Ethics stops being an adventure in which we try to become more and more like the image of God and becomes instead a series of gruelling tasks that must be carried out with white knuckles and plastered-on smiles. We go out into the world with blinders on, determined not to be led astray by its wiles. Down the *via dolorosa*, through the vale of tears, we climb until we reach our private Calvary. There, with consummate indifference, we nail ourselves to the nearest bit of crisscrossed wood and hang there, sure that each drop of suffering which spills from our tortured brow is a jewel in our heavenly crown. From the summit of our self-generated crucifixion, we look down on the poor, miserable sinners having fun in the streets below, and our souls wither under the weight of our jealousy.

This is very silly. The Law is for man, not man for the Law. Legalism is such a soul-draining practice that St. Paul likens it to being mad or under a spell (see Gal 3:1). If we think of our moral practices as something that we do in order to prove that we genuinely have the love of Jesus burning in our hearts then we've completely missed the point of the entire gospel. It is the love of Jesus burning in the heart that causes people to do good, not the other way around. This is the problem faced by the rich young man who approaches Christ in the gospel of Mark. It's a really poignant story: the young man has kept all of the commandments since his youth, but he feels on a gut level that it's not enough for him to inherit eternal life. He kneels before Jesus and asks to know what he must do. "Jesus looked steadily at him and loved him, and he said, 'There is one thing you lack. Go and sell everything you own and give the money to the poor, and you will have treasure in heaven; then come, follow me'" (Mark 10:21). The young man, misunderstanding, goes away sad.

The misunderstanding lies in the rich man's perception of Christ's calling. Christ is not saying, "There is one thing that you have failed to do for God." He is saying, "There is one thing you lack." He's not demanding something. He's offering. He sees this man perfectly, through the eyes of divine love, and sees what it is that's troubling his heart. He offers a solution. The young man receives it as a rebuke.

Poverty, properly understood, is not a negative practice. It's not a matter of getting rid of things, of denying oneself goods, of renouncing money. Poverty is not a lack of money, but a practice of freedom from the demands which money makes on people. It is creative. The rich young man could have asked himself, "How will I give my money to the poor? What is the most interesting and life-giving thing that I can do in order to rid myself of all this needless wealth? What sort of heavenly treasure might I invest in? What will Christ ask me to do once I have given up these riches in order to follow Him?"

The possibilities raised by the practice of poverty are richer than the pleasures and conveniences that can be bought. Poverty is an opportunity to engage with the world immediately, literally without the mediation of money. It challenges us to think of how we can use ourselves, our bodies, our talents in the service of God without having to rely on the narrow range of options which are available on the commodities market. It means that it becomes possible simply to go out and produce good and beautiful things without having to wait for someone else's *fiat*. The whole anxiety-ridden process of submitting the idea, waiting to see if it is accepted, whether the funding will come through, whether you'll be hired for the position, whether the work will meet with the approval of the marketing department flutters like a mirage and disappears. You don't have to wait for someone to hire you to look after the sick, you can just look after them. You needn't worry whether your art conforms to contemporary trends and fashions, you can simply make it. You don't have to comply with government guidelines in order to maintain tax-exempt status for your pro-life organization, you can just do what needs to be done. If the work is God's, the means will take care of themselves. If it's not God's, then it's not really worth doing anyway.

Of course this is the crux of our anxiety about money. There are things that we want to do, and we want them to succeed, regardless of whether they are worthwhile endeavors or not. Money serves to vouchsafe our freedom to undertake projects that God is not willing to invest in. Like Adam and Eve in the Beginning, we are afraid that the one tree that He refuses us will be the one tree that is able to bring us true happiness, and so we set about establishing the means by which to make sure that we are able to choose to eat from the branches of any tree in the garden.

But perhaps there is a greater fear underlying this. A fear that God does not actually have our best interests at heart. A fear that He is a hard and unjust master who expects to reap where He has not sown. We are so often afraid that if we turn our lives over to Him, He will not have compassion on our weakness, that He won't understand our incapacities, that He will demand of us more than we are capable of giving, and that He will not supply what we need. We might even imagine

119

this thought flickering across the mind of Eve when she reached towards the forbidden fruit: "I am called to be the image and likeness of God...and this fruit will make me like Him. Perhaps He has not given me the means to be myself. Perhaps I must claim them by my own efforts."

God understands these fears, and He will always be gentle with those who are suffering from them, but it is in order that we can live without such fear that He asks us to place ourselves in His hands, to trust Him. The surrender to divine providence involves allowing God the space to work, letting go of the reins a little bit in order that He can direct the chariot of the self towards whatever purpose He has planned for it. The soul that has embraced poverty becomes like a "feather on the breath of God," believing that His "power, working in us, can do infinitely more than we can ask or imagine" (Eph 3:20). By prying our eyes away from that one tantalizing fig that hangs on the bough of the forbidden tree we are enabled to see again that we live in a garden full of mysterious and beautiful fruits, all the work of our Creator, all pleasing, all good, all infused with the wisdom and glory of God.

About the Author

Melinda Selmys raises children, chickens and vegetables on a small farm in rural Ontario. The ghost of Elvis lives nearby. She is the author of *Sexual Authenticity: An Intimate Reflection on Homosexuality and Catholicism*, and blogs at sexualauthenticity.blogspot.com.

·

www.ingramcontent.com/pod-product-compliance
Lightning Source LLC
Chambersburg PA
CBHW071555040426
42452CB00008B/1185